PRAISE for MINDFUL LIVING

"OF ALL THE SPAS I've been associated with, Miraval is the only one that places such an emphasis on mindfulness and spirituality. It embodies the lifestyle practices that I teach and use myself, and truly offers a comprehensive experience of integrative medicine. The health practitioners and staff who work together at Miraval are an extraordinary team. *Mindful Living* gives you a glimpse of these highly skilled individuals and what they have to offer."

> **ANDREW WEIL,** M.D., world-renowned pioneer and leader in integrative medicine and *New York Times* best-selling author of *Healthy Aging* and *Spontaneous Healing*

"MIRAVAL'S WORLD-CLASS SPA RESORT has gifted readers with a holistic and integrative blueprint for optimal health and wellness. Transcendent meditations, luscious recipes, and invigorating physical movements form the *Mindful Living* template to achieve mental, spiritual, nutritional, and physical fitness. Each chapter brings more words of wisdom from an outstanding team of healers who will guide you in your own pursuit of a mindful life."

> **PAM PEEKE,** M.D., M.P.H., F.A.C.P., WebMD chief lifestyle expert; host of Discovery Health TV's *Could You Survive?*; and author of the *New York Times* bestsellers *Body for Life for Women, The Hunger Fix,* and *Fight Fat After Forty*

"MIRAVAL HAS BEEN PRAISED as one of the top spas in the world by many publications for many years. If anyone wonders why, they won't after reading this book. *Mindful Living* is brilliant. Mindfulness is not always an easy concept for people to grasp, yet it is one of the most powerful and scientifically proven stress reducers. By using the 12 months of the year as a guide and including exercises, treatments, and recipes, the reader comes away understanding mindfulness and has the tools to incorporate it into daily life. It is a marvelous thing that Miraval is sharing all its secrets in this well-written book. Lucky us."

> **SUSIE ELLIS,** President, SpaFinder Wellness

MINDFUL
LIVING

MIRAVAL RESORT & SPA HAS BEEN BLESSED WITH THE MOST AMAZING TEAM OF HEALERS, HEALTH PRACTITIONERS, WELLNESS PROVIDERS, AND STAFF WHO SPEND THEIR LIVES CREATING THE MAGIC OF BEING ABLE TO LIVE IN THE MOMENT. THIS BOOK IS A REFLECTION OF THEIR GIFTS. THEREFORE, MIRAVAL DEDICATES THIS BOOK TO OUR VALUED STAFF WITH SINCERE APPRECIATION.

MINDFUL LIVING

M|RAVAL®

HAY HOUSE, INC.
CARLSBAD, CALIFORNIA • NEW YORK CITY
LONDON • SYDNEY • JOHANNESBURG
VANCOUVER • HONG KONG • NEW DELHI

Published and distributed in the United States by: Hay House, Inc.:
www.hayhouse.com® • Published and distributed in Australia by:
Hay House Australia Pty. Ltd.: www.hayhouse.com.au • Published and distributed in
the United Kingdom by: Hay House UK, Ltd.: www.hayhouse.co.uk • Published and
distributed in the Republic of South Africa by: Hay House SA (Pty), Ltd.:
www.hayhouse.co.za • Distributed in Canada by: Raincoast: www.raincoast.com •
Published in India by: Hay House Publishers India: www.hayhouse.co.in

Produced by Stonesong
Cover and interior design: Vertigo Design NYC
Photography: Dana Gallagher, except the following pages
Courtesy of Miraval: x, xii, 4, 10, 14, 19, 26, 29, 32, 35 (lower), 44, 47, 48, 53
(upper, lower), 60 (left, right), 66, 67, 68, 69, 71, 78, 80, 83, 85, 93, 94, 100, 110,
113, 116, 117 (upper, lower), 124, 128, 133 (lower), 142, 143, 148, 149, 152–53, 157,
163, 165 (lower), 175, 177, 181 (upper, lower), 188, 190 (left, right), 193, 195
Graphics on pages 9, 17, 18: Courtesy of Kris Wright

Library of Congress Control Number: 2012946690

Hardcover ISBN: 978-1-4019-4200-7
Digital ISBN: 978-1-4019-4201-4

16 15 14 13   4 3 2 1
1st edition, May 2013

Printed in China

CONTENTS

A Note from the Owners   x

*A Note from Michael Tompkins,
Chief Executive Officer,
Miraval Resort & Spa*   xii

The Miraval Experience   xiii

Mindfulness   xiii

Mindful Living Month by Month   1

January | BEGINNINGS
featuring ANDREW WOLF   3

February | HEART
featuring ANNE PARKER   23

March | MEDITATION
featuring MARYGRACE NAUGHTON   41

April | WELLNESS
featuring JIM NICOLAI, M.D.   56

May | NUTRITION
featuring JUNELLE LUPIANI, R.D.   72

June | NATURE
featuring WYATT WEBB   89

July | CHALLENGE
featuring NEIL MCLEOD   105

August | OVERCOMING
OBSTACLES
featuring TIM FRANK, N.M.D.   121

September | HARVEST
featuring JUSTIN MACY   136

October | BALANCE
featuring LEIGH WEINRAUB   153

November | GRATITUDE
featuring PAM LANCASTER   169

December | CELEBRATION
featuring TEJPAL   184

Index of Recipes   204

Acknowledgments   206

A NOTE from the OWNERS

Our first visit to Miraval Resort & Spa, and every visit we've made since, has been a truly transformative experience. Miraval isn't simply a place to retreat and relax; it's a place where we get exposure to new ideas and learn new techniques for living a better, and more mindful, life. But we've always believed that the Miraval experience should not be limited to those of us who have the privilege to come to the resort in Tucson, and we've focused on opportunities to bring its life-changing experiences and lessons to more people and more places. By drawing from the incredible expertise of the Miraval team and specialists, *Mindful Living* will give you an opportunity to take the Miraval experience with you, no matter where you are.

STEVE AND JEAN CASE

A NOTE from MICHAEL TOMPKINS
Chief Executive Officer, Miraval Resort & Spa

For over 18 years, guests have been coming through the doors of Miraval. Many of them are seeking the classic "spa vacation" of rest and relaxation, while some come for the beauty of the desert setting, and others are looking for fun and adventure. All of our guests find these things at Miraval.

What most often surprises them is what they were *not* seeking—a variety of tools to assist in the expansion and improvement of their lives. Miraval has an innate power to gently magnify the best elements of who a person really is. How do I know this? Our guests tell me constantly in the conversations I've had with them, in the letters they write to me, and by their return visits to dip into this safe haven again and again.

What makes Miraval different from other spas comes down to one word: *mindfulness*. At other destination spas, it's often about "go, go, go" as guests dash from one activity to the next, generally focused on food and fitness and their desire to "get in shape" before their spa stay is through. At Miraval, we invite people to come through our gates and stop. It's not just about exercise—it's also about your breath, your spirit, your interactions with yourself and with others.

I see mindfulness as the realization that no matter where you are in life, you have the ability to tap into your breath and be completely in the present moment, thus allowing any decisions you make to be as positive and impactful as possible. All of the programs at Miraval share this focus: in fact, we even have a committee that evaluates every activity, from mountain biking to spa treatments, to ensure that each is built around the principle of mindfulness. The specialists who have been drawn to Miraval believe in these philosophies and live in the moment themselves. They want the experiences they share with our guests to be meaningful and authentic, and at Miraval it's all about the "we," not the "me." Our community of professionals work together to help you create a better life.

We feel this is the perfect time for this book, *Mindful Living*, which gives us a chance to share those tools with readers who have never been to Miraval as well as guests who are looking for ways to integrate their Miraval experience into their lives back home. So many people wish their lives away, focusing on some point in the future. "If I only had this, if I could only do that." At Miraval, we believe that every moment should be lived one at a time and appreciated for what it is. Even in difficult times, we have a choice as to how to react; and there is always an option for another, more mindful approach to the challenge at hand. It is our hope that we can help you find alternatives for healthy eating, stress reduction, living happily either with yourself or with a partner, and more fully enjoying every aspect of your life.

Welcome to Mindful Living,
MICHAEL

The MIRAVAL EXPERIENCE

There are spas . . . and then there is Miraval.

Miraval means "View of the Valley," a poignant name for this exclusive desert retreat nestled in the foothills of the Santa Catalina Mountains just north of Tucson, Arizona. And although some trips take you to places you've never been before, even to destinations that few others have ever seen, Miraval Resort & Spa offers the most inspiring getaway one can imagine—a journey unique to everyone who visits.

Consistently rated among the world's top spas and resorts by TripAdvisor and SpaFinder and publications such as *Travel+Leisure, Celebrated Living,* and *Condé Nast Traveler,* Miraval has earned its trendsetting reputation as America's destination for life betterment, where guests feel, are, and can be more.

Since its beginning in 1995, Miraval has upheld a powerfully simple vision: *Life is more meaningful and enjoyable when your physical, emotional, spiritual, social, and intellectual components are in balance.* To that end, Miraval offers more than 100 unique, life-enhancing programs and activities. Guests plan their stay filled with an abundance of choices, including innovative spa treatments, self-discovery activities led by insightful well-being specialists, dynamic growth and development programs, outdoor challenges, yoga and Pilates, stress-management techniques, and nutritional counseling. All aim to help people better manage our fast-paced world and life's daily demands.

Guests from around the world relish the resort not only for its luxury, but also for the deep comfort they can find nowhere else— speaking to Miraval's authentic wish for every guest: *You won't find you anywhere else.*
www.MiravalResorts.com

MINDFULNESS

Mindfulness is a term heard and seen often at Miraval, and it is the core concept that shapes Miraval's programs and environment.

Mindfulness is a conscious approach to being in the present moment—an elevated awareness of one's surroundings and also of oneself. It is a vivid perception of one's choices, strengths, and potential.

Mindfulness is empowering yourself and optimizing your energy in order to live a balanced, healthier, and better life, each and every day.

And just as Miraval guests are empowered by their experiences here and become able to make positive directional changes when they are at home, we hope that you, too, will be inspired by this book and what you learn from these pages.

MINDFUL LIVING MONTH by MONTH

The chapters of this book are set up to correspond to the 12 months of the year, with each month exploring a key tenet of the Miraval philosophy. A different Miraval specialist will provide insight on the featured subject; and each chapter will also contain an exercise, meditation, spa treatment, and recipe, all selected to help you explore the concept in more depth.

January, for example, focuses on beginnings with tips from Miraval's exercise physiologist on implementing an exercise program that will kick-start your health and weight-loss goals. The exercise section encourages you to begin each day with a morning stretch, while the spa section features a Flourish Body Scrub designed to reveal healthy new skin. Breathwalking is the perfect way to initiate a meditation practice, and the featured recipe is a seared diver-scallop appetizer that is bound to get your next meal off to a delicious, aromatic start.

But you certainly don't have to start with January or follow any particular sequence of steps. The cyclic design of the book allows you to leap in wherever you wish, so if your first priority is beginning a meditation program, flip to the March chapter and check out what Miraval's yoga and meditation department has to say about expanding your practice. Feeling like your life is a little off-kilter? Check out October where a Miraval specialist can help you see balance in a whole new way.

Mindful Living has many aspects and can be accessed through many doors. Just follow your instincts with an open mind and open heart and—most important of all—enjoy the journey!

January

BEGINNINGS In January, our minds naturally turn toward beginnings, perhaps in the form of New Year's resolutions. For a lot of us, this means pledges to exercise more, eat lighter, lose weight, and find better ways to deal with stress. The irresistibly clean slate of a new year makes January the perfect time to break old habits and introduce new ones.

YOUR EXERCISE PRESCRIPTION FOR WEIGHT LOSS

[EXPERT] *Andrew Wolf*

LOVE IT OR HATE IT, EXERCISE IS ONE OF THE KEY FACTORS IN OUR ABILITY TO LOSE WEIGHT AND KEEP IT OFF. BUT HOW MUCH EXERCISE DO WE NEED, AND WHAT'S THE MOST EFFECTIVE TYPE OF WORKOUT FOR WEIGHT LOSS?

"Managing your weight isn't necessarily about working out more," says exercise physiologist Andrew Wolf, M.Ed. "Sometimes it's a matter of working out smarter." At Miraval, Andrew leads classes titled Making Weight Loss a Reality, in which he clears up fitness myths, and

Prevention and Metabolism, which explores how exercise can help prevent conditions such as coronary artery disease, diabetes, and hypertension. He also works individually with clients in his Optimal Fitness Diagnostic program, where he collects data on their maximum heart rates, aerobic capacity, blood pressure, and medical history in order to write an individualized "exercise prescription."

Many of the people who show up in Andrew's office have been on dozens of diets and are already working out at least occasionally, but they're still struggling with their weight. Perhaps that's because they're carrying not just excess body fat, but also several misconceptions about exercise.

"Weight loss is more about diet than exercise.
 I think I saw that on the cover of *Time*, right?"

Successful weight loss almost always requires you to make adjustments in both your food intake and level of exercise. It's true, the diet part of the equation tends to move the scale faster in the beginning, but the positive effects of exercise are cumulative. In other words, the more efficient you become at working out, the bigger an impact exercise begins to have on your ability to lose weight. The problem is that many people jump on the exercise bandwagon, don't find the quick results they want, and then jump back off before they've built their aerobic capacity to the point where they would have begun seeing real improvement.

One of the reasons weight loss is so frustrating is that, at least on the surface, the math is simple: If you take in 1,500 calories a day through food, but burn 2,000 calories through activity, you've created a 500-calorie deficit for that day.

Over the course of a week that's a 3,500-calorie deficit, and since 3,500 calories equates to one pound of body fat, a person who creates a 500-calorie deficit each day will lose a pound a week. Keep it up for a year, and that's a whopping 52 pounds of fat loss.

It may be simple, but it sure isn't easy—or else why would we have so much trouble doing it? And why would there be so many diets out there, each claiming something contradictory?

"The diet industry is huge, and it plays a lot of games," says Andrew. "Diets that limit carbohydrates promise you'll lose far more than a pound a week, but what they don't tell you is that those pounds are mostly water, not fat. Every gram of carbohydrate has three to four grams of water associated with it. When you stop eating them in your diet, your body begins to deplete all the carbohydrates that

were stored as glycogen in your liver and muscles, and a lot of water comes out with it. Losing ten pounds in two weeks may make people happy in the short run, but they can't sustain it." Low-calorie diets can be just as bad, sometimes forcing dieters to restrict calories so drastically that it's nearly impossible for them to meet their nutritional needs.

Junelle Lupiani, R.D., is the nutritionist at Miraval, and she often works with Andrew to create weight-loss plans for guests. "Sometimes we meet a person who says, 'I'm not crazy about exercise and I'm not going to do it, so just tell me what I need to eat,'" Junelle says. "Or, on the flip side, they'll say, 'Look, I love my nachos and cheese dip too much to give them up, so just tell me how much I have to exercise to offset them.' Both of those people are going to have a very hard time losing weight. What works best is a two-pronged approach: eat a little less and move a little more."

MYTH #2

"I just need to fire up my metabolism."

"People starting a weight-loss program often have the false idea that they need to increase their metabolism," says Andrew. "There's only one problem with that: Your metabolic rate is largely out of your control."

Here's why: Your RMR, or resting metabolic rate, equals the number of calories you'd burn in 24 hours if you did absolutely nothing but lie on the couch. In other words, it's the number of calories it takes to keep your body functioning in terms of respiration, heartbeat, digestion, and growing new cells. Just as your power bill depends on the size of the building you're heating, the amount of energy it takes to maintain the basic functions of a human body is largely tied to the size of that body. It costs a lot more calories to run a 6'5" basketball player than it takes to sustain a 5'4" woman.

The fact that our metabolism is so closely related to the size of our bodies is also the basis of one of the cruel jokes of nature—that is, as we lose weight, it gets progressively harder to keep losing weight. Since it took more energy to maintain a 200-pound body than a 150-pound one, the resting metabolic rate of a successful dieter actually slows as her waistline shrinks. This is one reason why it's so hard to drop those last ten pounds.

"Since there's so little we can do about our RMR, I advise people not to worry about it," Andrew says. "We need to focus on what we can control, which is the number of calories we burn through exercise. And that means cardio."

MYTH #3

"The amount of lean body mass I have has a huge impact on how many calories I burn, even at rest. So I need to start lifting weights immediately."

"Most women have about 100 pounds of lean body mass and most men about 140," Andrew says. "What makes us look so different from each other is how much fat we carry. We all have six-pack abs; it's just that some of us are doing a great job of hiding them with a layer of belly fat."

You've probably heard that weight training builds lean body mass, which in turn increases your metabolism and ultimately how many calories you burn in a typical day. That's all true, but pumping iron doesn't affect your weight loss nearly as much as you may think.

One *Medicine and Science in Sports and Exercise* study followed people who did heavy weight training for 24 weeks. They all gained muscle mass, but only the men saw a resultant bump in their metabolic rate. The women burned an average of 47 more calories a day. At that rate, it would take you 74 days to lose a pound!

For people who want to lose weight, Andrew suggests they focus not on building muscle but rather on keeping what they already have. The

Morning Stretch

Many Miraval guests opt to begin their day with a morning stretch, and Pam Trudeau, fitness director of the Bodymindfulness Center, says there are significant benefits to the practice. "After several hours of sleeping, your muscles can become stiff and tight," says Pam, "so taking some time first thing in the morning to stretch will increase blood flow to those muscles, release tension, and perhaps even eliminate back pain."

To avoid risking injury by overstretching a cold muscle, Pam suggests you spend a few minutes prior to your stretch warming up. "Walk out to get the newspaper or to let the dogs out," she says. "A warm-up can be as simple as rolling your shoulders, doing a few arm circles, or shaking out your legs. Or you could begin your morning-stretch routine after a warm bath or shower."

An ideal morning stretch focuses on the major muscle groups: neck, shoulders, low back, hips, thighs,

and calves. It can be sequenced from head to toe, or you might want to start with the area of your body that, as Pam says, "happens to be speaking to you the loudest." For many people, this will be the hips or low back. Since the ultimate goal of stretching is to increase your mobility while in motion, an "active stretch" where, for example, you slowly rock in and out of a calf stretch gradually increasing your range of motion, may be more beneficial than a static stretch, where you move directly into a full position and hold it for a minute.

Although the Miraval Morning Stretch is a 45-minute class that systematically addresses every part of the body, Pam says that shorter sessions have benefits as well. "You can reduce stiffness and improve your posture with two or three 15-minute stretch sessions a week," she says. "And working in a few stretches at your computer or desk is a great way to relieve stress."

amount of weight training required to maintain muscle mass is quite modest: Andrew estimates a 15- to 30-minute session twice a week will do it. "You can have a trainer show you a short but effective circuit at your local gym," he says. "The trainer might try to convince you that you need more, but if weight loss is your goal, you want to do the bare minimum of weight training needed and spend that extra time in cardio. If you prefer, your two weight-training sessions can be at home with free

weights. Yoga, Pilates, or those boot-camp workouts with push-ups and squats work as well."

The amount of weight training in Andrew's prescription may be minimal, but it's not skippable. We're all in danger of losing muscle as we age, especially women who are approaching or have gone through menopause. Cutting calories puts us at even higher risk, because our bodies are smart and, in fact, strategic. Once your body realizes it's getting fewer calories

than it's used to, it will begin looking around for something it can afford to unload. If you haven't used your triceps in the last three months, your body will quite logically conclude you don't need that muscle very much and will begin to devour it instead of the harder-to-metabolize roll of fat around your waist.

So weight training is vital to keep what you have, but the point is you don't have to go as long or as hard as you may have been led to believe. "One weight-training session a week begins to protect the muscle," says Andrew. "Two is better. But after that it's a matter of diminishing returns. Eighty to 90 percent of the benefits of weight training can be gotten in two sessions a week, so the advantages gained by adding a third are slight."

GETTING MORE BANG for YOUR CARDIO BUCK by INCREASING YOUR AEROBIC CAPACITY

When it comes to weight loss, nothing beats a nice, sweaty, heart-pumping cardio workout. And what really has an effect on how many calories you burn during exercise is a rarely discussed little thing called "aerobic capacity."

Aerobic capacity (sometimes called VO2 max) refers to how many liters of oxygen you consume during a single minute of working out, which is a function of how efficient your heart is at pumping blood. While studies don't reveal a remarkable range of lean body mass or resting metabolic rate among healthy adult women, there's a much larger range in their aerobic capacity. Increasing this capacity means you'll be less winded at the top of a flight of stairs and can shave a few minutes off your 10K time . . . but when it comes to weight loss, the real benefit of increased aerobic capacity is that you'll burn more calories each time you work out.

Luckily, we have a lot of control over this number. In fact, expanding our aerobic capacity may be the single biggest thing we can do to increase our weight loss through exercise.

Andrew finds that the majority of his Optimal Fitness Diagnostic clients fit a certain prototype, and he affectionately calls them his "two-liter ladies." When a two-liter lady is working as hard as she can on a treadmill, she's consuming two liters of oxygen per minute and burning ten calories in the effort.

Of course, few people can sustain an all-out pace for long. When the two-liter lady is back home in her gym, she's generally working out at closer to 70 percent of her aerobic capacity; 70 to 80 percent of our maximum heart rate is often dubbed the "aerobic zone" and is a level of intensity where we definitely are aware we're working out, but at a pace we can comfortably sustain for a while. At 70 percent of

her maximum, our two-liter lady is burning about 7 calories a minute. So if she spends 30 minutes on the treadmill, she'll burn 210 calories.

Not bad, but not great. If this same woman can improve her aerobic capacity to 2.8 liters, she will burn 10 calories a minute, which means that same 30-minute treadmill walk at 70 percent effort now earns her 300 calories. Therefore, it's easy to see how, over time, increased aerobic capacity can make a huge difference in the number of calories burned in exercise, thus making our training far more efficient.

So how does the two-liter lady become the 2.8-liter lady?

"The heart is a strong and stubborn muscle," Andrew says. "We rarely use our triceps, for example, so just a little bit of effort will wake them up. But our heart is beating all the time, even when we sleep. It's already used to constant work, so to get its attention you have to do something drastic."

INTERVAL TRAINING, or "THE REVENGE
of the TWO-LITER LADY"

The "drastic" thing Andrew is talking about is interval training.

But before you yawn and say, "But I'm already doing that in spinning class," keep reading. This isn't your typical interval training.

Most people think of interval training as a cycle in which they slightly elevate and then slightly decrease their heart rate—like a spinning class where you pedal fast for four minutes, recover for 30 seconds between songs, and then speed up again.

Andrew advocates a much more significant interval, a cycle he describes as "gnarly," meaning an intense segment during which you're working at a pace that simply wouldn't be sustainable for longer than a couple of minutes. (In the beginning, before you acclimate to this kind of training, you may not even be able to sustain it for two minutes.) The intense interval is followed by what Andrew calls "a ridiculously easy recovery. The sort of pace where if anyone you knew came in the gym and caught you going that slowly, you'd be embarrassed."

So if your usual interval training looks like this:

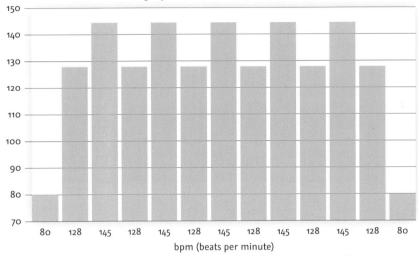

TYPICAL INTERVAL
Heart rate (bpm) is going back and forth between a comfortable 75% and a slightly uncomfortable 85% of heart-rate max

Your aerobic-capacity training intervals would look more like this:

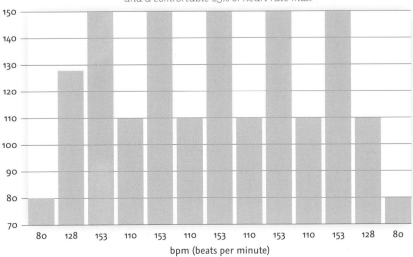

EFFECTIVE INTERVAL
Heart rate (bpm) is going back and forth between a "gnarly" 90% and a comfortable 65% of heart-rate max

Breathwalking

Can two things as simple as breathing and walking really provide the same benefits as meditation? Absolutely, especially if you synchronize them into a technique known as breathwalking.

"Our default breathing is not ideal for health," says Dr. Jim Nicolai, Medical Director of the Andrew Weil, M.D., Integrative Wellness Program at Miraval. "For many of us, our 'normal' breath is rapid and shallow in the chest; and since our automatic nervous system reflects our state of mind, this shallow breathing signals our body to stay turned on, stressed, and in a constant state of mild anxiety." Fortunately, the principle works just as well in reverse. "If we begin to breathe fuller, deeper, and more from the abdomen," says Dr. Jim, "we automatically activate a sense of calm."

The secret of breathwalking is to synchronize your steps with your breaths, linking one breath with each step. A Kundalini yoga technique, it's great for people who struggle with seated meditation, those with

twitchy bodies and busy minds. "Some people find it easier to relax in motion," says Dr. Jim. "So breath-walking works well for those who aren't 'the medita-tion type.' And since you can practice it while walking the dog or running errands, breathwalking takes no extra time from your day."

There are two basic techniques in breathwalking, the Wave and the Stairs, and both are built on a four-in, four-out pattern. With the Wave, you breathe in through your nose for a count of four, meanwhile taking four steps, then breathe out through your mouth for another count of four, while taking four more steps. Since it takes eight beats to complete one inhalation and exhalation, the Wave automatically slows your breathing, but you may have to focus a little more to deepen your breath.

"We've been taught to suck our bellies in, and this learned posture has contributed to the American epi-demic of shallow breathing," says Dr. Jim. "One way to trick yourself into deeper breaths is to consciously pull your belly in on the final beat of your exhalation, bringing your navel toward your spine. Then on the first beat of your inhale, you'll automatically push your belly back out and the breath can go deeper."

While the Wave is designed for relaxation, the Stairs pattern is more energizing. This time there are four distinct in breaths, followed by four distinct out breaths. It may take some practice to get the four segments even, but when you do it sounds a bit like Lamaze breathing, and the Stairs can take you to a state Dr. Jim describes as "active calm."

"If you're getting drowsy midday, go for a walk and do the Stairs breathing," says Dr. Jim, "or if you're stressed at work, do the Wave at your desk. The Wave is also great for settling the brain and helping you to fall asleep at night. If practiced regularly, both techniques have the power to change your default mode, making your breaths deeper and more even throughout the whole day."

There's good news and bad news about this program. The bad news is that the pace during the intense part of the intervals will be 86 to 92 percent of your maximum heart rate, and two minutes in that zone won't be easy. The good news is that the recovery between intervals will be complete, dropping your heart rate down to the 60 percent range where you can rest and regroup before beginning the next interval. The even better news is that you only have to do this interval workout twice a week.

Intervals can be done during any kind of workout you prefer, but Andrew suggests a treadmill, rower, stationary bike, or elliptical machine where you can easily adjust the speed, incline, or resistance to get your heart rate to exactly where you need it to be. Since this program requires you to

hit specific heart rates during both the intervals and the recovery, you'll also need a heart-rate monitor. Andrew cautions that the heart-rate readouts provided by the machines are often inaccurate, so invest in your own monitor. A simple wristwatch-style model with a strap that runs across your chest will be about $50, available online and at sporting and department stores.

The protocol looks like this: a long, slow warm-up; then your first interval; followed by a period of recovery before the next interval. Repeat the cycle five times and then finish with a long, slow cooldown.

Theoretically you could be spending only ten minutes per session at the highest heart-rate level, but few novices have the aerobic capacity to maintain a full two minutes at 86 to 92 percent of

their maximum heart rate when they begin. "It may take you awhile to work up to this," Andrew says, "especially if you're not used to exercising this intensely. Beginners often need to start with intervals that last four to six minutes at a heart rate of more like 80 percent of their max, then 85 percent. This means, of course, that in their initial weeks of training, it might take them longer to get five intervals into a single workout. But gradually, they can work up to the super intense two-minute intervals."

The payoff of interval training is that your heart pumps more blood, uses more oxygen, and thus burns more calories. The longer the training continues, the better your heart will get at reaching new levels of aerobic capacity and the more calories you'll burn.

HOW HARD IS HARD?

Obviously this is a hard workout, but exactly how hard?

Your heart-rate goals for both the top of the interval and the recovery are based on percentages of your maximum heart rate. While many people still rely on the old formula of subtracting your age from 220, Andrew says this often

doesn't work. An active 50-year-old might be more fit than a sedentary 30-year-old, so it's risky to estimate your maximum based exclusively on your age.

You can learn your true maximum heart rate in several ways.

One way is to have an Optimal Fitness Diagnostic, such as the one

offered at Miraval, which will give you all of the information you need for efficient training. Lacking that, you can have a stress test administered by your doctor. (If you're over 50, the cost may be covered by insurance.) Once you know your maximum, you can figure out what 86 to 92 percent of that number is and will thus be able to determine the range you're aiming for at the top of the interval as well as your 60 percent recovery.

In order to get a true sense of their maximum heart rate during a test, Andrew urges clients "not to hang on the treadmill bars, but to give it all you have, as if you're being chased by wild dogs. Unless you determine your absolute max, you won't be able to accurately set your intervals, and you may be cheating yourself from getting the most possible out of all your later workouts."

If you don't have access to fitness diagnostic or stress tests, don't despair. Andrew says there's another way to estimate your maximum. "When left to their own devices, most people exercise at 75 percent of their heart rate," he says. "So go to your usual spinning class or get on the elliptical machine. Then after 30 minutes, check your heart rate. If it's 140, for example, then you can figure that your maximum is about 186."

WORKING the NUMBERS

Once you know your target heart-rate range, the workout might go something like this. Let's say your maximum heart rate is 180, which is typical of a lot of the clients Andrew tests. Your 70 to 80 percent "cruising speed" range will be 126 to 144. That's the heart rate you're probably exercising at now—one that feels, if not exactly comfortable, at least like a level of exertion you can maintain for 20 or 30 minutes. "This is a good rate for a sustained workout, and sustained workouts should be part of your overall exercise program," says Andrew. "But don't kid yourself into thinking this is an interval, even if you bounce around between 126 and 144 during the workout."

To reach your true interval range of 86 to 92 percent, you'll need to elevate your heart rate to between 154 and 166. After each interval comes a cooldown, where you allow your heart to return gradually to 60 percent of its max. So if your maximum heart rate is 180, your cooldown would be 108.

For many people, intervals at 86 to 92 percent will feel much more intense than they're used to. (Remember what Andrew said about taking time to work up to this range.) You may opt to begin with intervals of six minutes at 80 percent of your max or a heart rate of 144. After you've done several workouts at this pace, switch to four-minute intervals at 149. Gradually, you should be able to handle two minutes at a heart rate of 154 to 166.

"It sounds counterintuitive to go longer when you're just beginning, but the less fit a person is, the longer and less intense the interval needs to be," says Andrew. "By cranking it up gradually, you can build your confidence and stamina over time as you're also improving the condition of your blood vessels and increasing your aerobic capacity."

But whether you're doing shorter intervals or longer, the same pattern still holds—a long, slow warm-up; five cycles of intervals and recovery; and then a long, slow cooldown.

It's important to acknowledge that these intervals are designed to be hard. The purpose of them is to challenge your heart, which is quite comfortable with certain levels or work, to go into uncomfortable levels and thus be forced to pump more blood. If all you're doing is rearranging your existing workout, your heart won't increase its aerobic capacity, and you won't get the ultimate payoff, which is the ability to burn more calories during all exercise. "If 90 percent of your max is 162, you're not going to be happy at 162," Andrew says, "but the point is, you're not supposed to be happy at 162."

This is also why it's essential to use a heart-rate monitor rather than relying on your own perceived rate of exertion. Perceived rate of exertion may be an adequate gauge in a workout you're familiar with, such as a dance class you take every week, but these intervals probably represent an unexplored heart-rate territory. If you've rarely taken your heart rate above 75 percent of its maximum before, it's unlikely you'll be able to perceive the difference between 80 percent and 85 percent. They'll just seem like two variations of "very hard."

"People often overestimate how hard they're working, and gym machines overestimate it, too," says Andrew. "A heart-rate monitor keeps you honest and serves as your coach in absentia. There's not always going to be an exercise physiologist or trainer hanging over you, urging you to work harder than you want to. The monitor is our proxy."

Another note: Even as your fitness level gradually improves, the goal numbers will stay the same, at least until your next cardio evaluation. "If your target during an interval is 162, the amount of work it takes to get you to 162 may change over time," says Andrew. "You'll find yourself increasing the speed or the resistance on the machine. But the goal is still 162."

You should only do this interval workout twice a week. "More is not

better with intervals," says Andrew. "These are tough workouts, and if you try to do them too often, you'll put yourself at risk for mental burnout and overuse injuries."

He also recommends that you do the interval workout for three months at a time, and then take a break from it for a month before starting back. "People speak of maintaining fitness as if it were a matter of doing the same thing week in and week out," Andrew says. "The reality is that maintaining is more about boosting your fitness to a new level, then taking a break and letting it fall back a bit. Then boost it, and let it fall back again."

Okay, so the prescription now includes two interval sessions a week and two weight-training sessions, but what do you do the rest of the time?

WHAT a PERFECT WEEK of EXERCISE LOOKS LIKE

The two sessions of interval training stand on their own as workouts. But the 15- to 30-minute weight-training sessions can be combined with 30 to 45 minutes of moderate-intensity cardio exercise, such as a dance or spinning class at your gym or perhaps just a brisk walk through the neighborhood. Four days of cardio a

week, including the intervals, is the minimum prescription for weight loss. You can certainly do more.

"Ideally, you throw as many exercise variations at yourself as you can in the course of a week," says Andrew. "You might want to add one session of long, slow distance on a weekend, such as a hike or

bike ride. If you're less concerned about weight loss, you can add more weight training or something like yoga or Pilates. But if weight loss is your primary goal, keep your additional exercise sessions cardio based and include a variety of sustained moderate-intensity workouts."

SPA
Flourish Body Scrub

A body scrub is an especially good treatment for the winter months, when dead skin cells tend to accumulate. After an exfoliation, you may be extra vulnerable to the sun and wind, so take precautions to protect your fresh, baby-soft skin.

How can I do this at home?

ORGANIC FLOURISH BODY SCRUB Pamper and purify your skin at home with this easy-to-make salt or sugar scrub, which will stimulate circulation, detoxify, firm, and soften your skin.

HOME CARE Using a floral-scented massage oil of your choice, take a ½ cup of sea salt or granulated sugar and add just enough oil to make it pliable but not too oily (for safety reasons!). Apply in a gentle circular motion onto dry or moist skin while in the shower. Rinse off and pat skin dry. Finish with a similar scented body butter to lock in the moisture. This body beauty ritual can be done every two weeks to keep your skin revitalized, renewed, and radiantly flourishing. Miraval uses the following Red Flower organic floral essential oil—derived body oils for customized benefits:

FRENCH LAVENDER regenerative nutrients; skin-cell renewal to repair damaged/aging skin

ICELANDIC MOONFLOWER euphoria-inducing; vitamin-rich antioxidant; intensely hydrating

INDIAN JASMINE intense, night scent; deeply nourishing skin; healing and purifying

JAPANESE PEONY highly absorbent and penetrating moisture; potent antioxidants

MOROCCAN ROSE increasing elasticity, minimizing fine lines; repairing damaged skin cells

What better way to do "out with the old, in with the new" than with a customized body scrub? The Miraval Flourish Body Scrub is designed to remove dead skin cells and then hydrate, firm, and soften the skin beneath.

The service begins with guests selecting their favorite scent from a variety of pleasurable options. Each is infused with sea algae, protein, and vitamin-rich antioxidants, all of which stimulate circulation and detoxify impurities within the skin.

The spa therapist uses a mortar and pestle to blend your choice of scent with sea salt, and the mixture is then brushed on the skin. If you've experienced aggressive "sand blast" exfoliations in the past, you'll be amazed by this gentle process. After the exfoliation, you'll shower with a botanical gel in your chosen scent, and then return to the table for a light massage with organic oil.

THE MAGIC 2,000

Studies indicate you need to burn 2,000 calories a week through exercise in order to lose weight and keep it off. (And, as we'll later see, this same magic number can also protect you from a variety of diseases.) There are many ways to expend 2,000 calories in the course of a week. For example, you burn approximately 100 calories a mile whether you're walking it at 3 mph in 20 minutes or running it at 6 mph in 10. So to burn 2,000 calories in a walking/running program, you'll need to cover 20 miles a week.

If your fitness level is such that you need to start with a slow, easy pace, like 3 mph, it will take you a longer time to burn the necessary calories—approximately an hour of walking a day or 400 minutes a week. If you can increase your pace to 4 mph, you'll cover that 20 miles in 5 hours of walking a week and cut your workout time per day to 42 minutes.

But the real time-saving benefit kicks in with increased levels of aerobic capacity, which is one of the reasons Andrew believes interval training to be such an integral part of a weight-loss plan. "A lot of people simply don't have an hour to work out every day," he says.

"They're trying to burn that 2,000 calories as efficiently as possible, so if they can increase their aerobic capacity to the point where they're burning ten calories a minute, no matter what exercise they're using to burn them, they can reach that magic 2,000 in 200 minutes a week. You've just cut the amount of time you have to work out in half because you're talking four workouts of 50 minutes each, which is much more doable for a lot of people than an hour every day. Increased aerobic capacity not only improves the strength of your heart, but it also makes it easier to meet your weight-loss goals in minimal time, which ultimately makes you more likely to stick with the program."

HOW DO YOU BEGIN?

A lot of people see January as the ideal month to start or accelerate an exercise program, but Andrew warns that "while there's nothing wrong with New Year's resolutions per se, you don't want to go haywire and try to introduce too many changes at once. The bolder a move you try to make, the higher the chance that the pendulum will eventually swing in the other direction."

Rather than attempting to morph from a couch potato to extreme athlete in one month—and risk ending back up on the couch—Andrew suggests you "break your exercise goals into small pieces and achieve those pieces one at a time. Introduce one new behavior in January, even if that feels like an underwhelming change, and spend the month making it a habit. Then in February, introduce something else."

Consider adding the intervals first. "When a woman who is in or approaching menopause comes to me," Andrew says, "she may complain about a decline in energy or stamina, but she often doesn't realize the total effect this is having on the efficiency of her workouts and in turn her weight. Perhaps when she was in her 20s she could go to the gym, work out hard, and burn 12 calories a minute. Now she feels like she's working just as hard as ever, but due to declining aerobic capacity she's only burning 6 calories a minute. Her weight is creeping up, and she's frustrated. In these cases, the interval training is often the missing piece of the puzzle and the obvious first thing to fix."

It takes about three weeks to begin seeing changes in your aerobic capacity or losses on the scale. "People sometimes get frustrated because when their fitness levels are low, as they often are at the beginning of an exercise program, they can't work out very hard," says Andrew, "which is a bummer because the amount of stimulus you can throw at yourself is less, and thus you don't necessarily see quick results. In the first month, you may feel like you're banging your head against a wall, and it may seem like exercise isn't that helpful for weight loss. But as you get fitter, you'll be able to work out harder, and you'll definitely see the results."

BE REALISTIC

Another potential problem with a dramatic New Year's resolution is that you may be tempted to aim for an unrealistic goal weight.

"For a lot of people their ideal weight is tied to a certain time in their lives," Andrew says. "Back when they were jocks in college or before they got married and had kids. A woman might look at a picture of herself standing on a beach in a bikini and think something like, *I weighed 125 pounds then, and that's what I need to get back to*. But that's a fantasy weight."

Andrew considers basing your goal weight on the BMI formula nearly as problematic as nostalgia. "BMI doesn't distinguish between a bicep and a love handle," he says. "A woman may have looked great at 125 when she was 20, but now, two decades and three kids later, she probably has more butt muscle, more thigh muscle. And if she were somehow able to get back to that 125 she would have to lose a lot of that muscle to do it. She wouldn't look like that picture on the beach. She'd be gaunt and scary skinny."

Most of the people Andrew tests have a body-fat percentage between 28 percent and 42 percent, considerably higher than the recommended percentages of 20 to 28 percent for women and 13 to 18 percent for men. Thus, they do need to lose body fat but precisely how much is a figure that should be adjusted as they proceed along their weight-loss journey. "The woman who weighed 125 in her 20s may be fit, healthy, and comfortable at 140 in her 40s," says Andrew.

But, this doesn't mean the old picture of the woman on a beach in her bikini is useless. If it's the impetus that gets her to start exercising again, that picture may ultimately save her from diabetes or hypertension.

EXERCISE and DISEASE PREVENTION

"When people come in and say they want an exercise plan that will help them lose weight in the next six months, I give it to them," says Andrew, "because I have a sneaky ulterior motive. By doing these things to lose weight, they'll also automatically be decreasing their risk of getting a variety of preventable lifestyle-influenced diseases."

Scientists who study the correlation between exercise and disease have zeroed in on the precise dose-response relationship for three major diseases that affect millions of Americans: hypertension (high blood pressure), diabetes, and coronary artery disease. "It's important to know just how much exercise you need to create the benefit," says Andrew. "Just like in medication, you're looking for the lowest effective dose."

HYPERTENSION

If you look at the chart below, you'll quickly notice the best thing about exercise and hypertension: You don't have to do much to start seeing the benefits. By burning 1,000 calories a week in exercise, you reduce your risk of hypertension, or if you've already been diagnosed

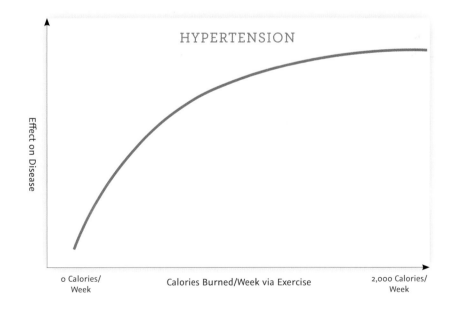

HYPERTENSION

Effect on Disease

0 Calories/ Week   Calories Burned/Week via Exercise   2,000 Calories/ Week

with high blood pressure, you can begin to reverse the condition.

The exercise can be done at any pace you wish. Walking does the trick; or if you prefer, you can put the time in on a rower, elliptical machine, or in an exercise class. The one caveat is that the exercise time needs to be spread out over multiple sessions. People seeking to reduce their risk of hypertension can't be weekend warriors who do massive amounts of exercise on Saturday and Sunday but are idle the rest of the week. Shorter, more frequent exercise sessions are the key.

The same regime reduces your level of stress, which is not only closely linked to hypertension but other conditions as well, including insomnia, depression, and anxiety. Some studies suggest regular exercise can also push back the onset of dementia, perhaps delaying the symptoms as much as ten years. To get the stress-reducing benefits of exercise, you don't have to crack the whip in long, hard workouts. A daily 20-minute walk will suffice.

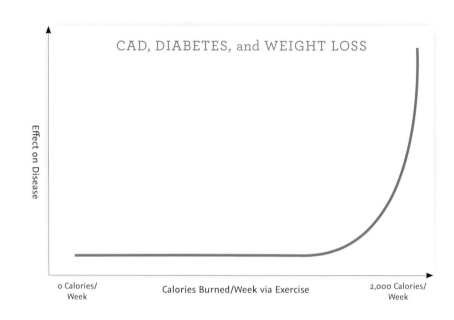

CORONARY ARTERY DISEASE (CAD) and DIABETES

To reduce your chances of getting coronary artery disease or diabetes, or to reverse the conditions if you've already been diagnosed, you need to burn 2,000 calories a week in exercise. It's possible for weekend warriors to get the coronary-artery benefit with extended workouts like distance bike rides or hikes. Diabetes, in contrast, is more of a "What have you done for me lately?" type of disease, requiring several exercise sessions a week.

As long as your weekly efforts total 2,000 calories burned, you get the same benefits for diabetes and coronary artery disease whether you exercise in long, slow sessions or shorter, harder ones. But since 2,000 calories requires a lot of exercise,

"Weight loss is just the happy side effect of doing the things you already should be doing to increase your chances of a long and healthy life."

those with time demands will find themselves once again turning back to the need to increase their aerobic capacity.

"Some of my clients are happy with their weight but come to me because they've just been diagnosed, had a health scare, or have a family history of a condition like diabetes," says Andrew. "These people are highly motivated, but when we get into specifics, we often end up having the same conversations I have with my clients who are seeking weight loss. They realize they need to increase their aerobic capacity in order to burn the 2,000 calories in an efficient amount of time."

No matter what your initial motivation for doing it, exercise has a profound impact on your overall health. "If you're following the workout prescription described previously for weight loss, you're already burning enough calories to protect yourself from hypertension, diabetes, and coronary artery disease," says Andrew. "Weight loss is just the happy side effect of doing the things you already should be doing to increase your chances of a long and healthy life."

KEY POINTS FOR JANUARY

✿ The best way for an exercise program to aid in your weight-loss efforts is with interval training. Your workouts should rotate between extremely challenging intervals done at 90 percent of your maximum heart rate and complete recovery intervals that allow your heart rate to drop to 65 percent of its maximum.

✿ To take weight off and keep it off, you'll need to burn 2,000 calories a week through exercise.

✿ Exercise also plays a key role in the prevention of hypertension, diabetes, coronary artery disease, and stress.

ANDREW WOLF, Exercise Physiologist, M.Ed., R.C.E.P.

Andrew earned a master's degree in kinesiology from the University of Texas at Austin's Human Performance Lab and an accreditation as a registered clinical physiologist. He has accumulated more than 12 years of experience writing exercise prescriptions. He has also cultivated wide-ranging interests in exercise for disease prevention and the treatment of diseases such as diabetes, heart disease, and hypertension. From competitive triathlete to the person using an integrated approach to disease prevention, Andrew has the experience and training to prescribe exercise for every need.

PAN-SEARED DIVER SCALLOP with PURPLE POTATOES, CHIVES, and WHITE TRUFFLE OIL

The best meals start with appetizers, those luscious little bites that signal to our minds and bodies that it's time to unplug from the workday and relax into a time of sharing and celebration. But many restaurant appetizers are calorie bombs—deep fried, overly sauced, and laden with cheese and cream. The Pan-Seared Diver Scallop below is an appetizer done right. Visually beautiful and incredibly decadent—it even has white truffle oil!—it's a light but satisfying start to a festive dinner.

MAKES 4 SERVINGS

4 large diver scallops (fresh sea scallops, approximately 1 ounce each)

½ c. whipped purple potatoes

1 tsp. white truffle oil

2 fresh chive stems each cut into 1½" lengths

1 tsp. extra-virgin olive oil

Pinch kosher salt

Pinch freshly ground black pepper

WHIPPED POTATOES

1 medium purple potato, peeled and sliced

2 tsp. extra-virgin olive oil

⅛ tsp. kosher salt

⅛ tsp. freshly ground black pepper

FOR THE POTATOES: Place the potato in a medium saucepan with enough cold water to cover by 1 inch, and bring to a boil over high heat. Reduce the heat and cook at a low boil until the potato is fork tender but not falling apart, 17 to 20 minutes.

Drain the potato well, place in a medium bowl, and mash with a potato masher. (Alternatively, turn the potato through a ricer into a bowl.) Stir in the olive oil, salt, and pepper; and mix well.

FOR THE SCALLOPS: Season the scallops lightly on both sides with the salt and pepper.

Heat a clean medium sauté pan over high heat until hot. Add olive oil and swirl to coat the bottom of the pan. Add the scallops and cook until well seared, about 1½ minutes. Turn the scallops over and continue cooking until well seared, about 1 minute. Remove pan from heat.

TO PLATE: Spoon about 2 tablespoons of the whipped potatoes onto a small plate. Place a scallop against the potato, drizzle with ¼ teaspoon white truffle oil, and garnish with 2 pieces of chive. Serve immediately.

CALORIES: 75; TOTAL FAT: 2 G; CARBOHYDRATES: 6 G; DIETARY FIBER: TRACE; PROTEIN: 7 G

February

HEART February is all about hearts, whether the love comes in the form of cardiovascular health, romance, or extending blessings to the world at large. This month we'll look at how we can maintain our personal balance and joy no matter what's going on around us, even when those we love may be struggling. We'll also look at how our emotional needs change throughout life and how to know when it's time for a little personal reinvention. Most of us let our heads do the choosing, but if we can remember to follow our hearts sometimes as well, they can lead us to new and unexpected places.

to see the advantages of your new situation: a less expensive house, a better climate, a more satisfying job, and a school system that will ultimately give your daughter a better education once she adapts to its higher demands.

"Life is rarely static and resolved," says Anne. "There's almost always something that is bothering us or someone we love. Many of these problems are completely beyond our control because they involve another person's thoughts, emotions, and actions.

The challenge for the mother is to acknowledge that her daughter is discontented, do what she can to love and support her, and still make the choice to be happy herself."

Does the very idea that a mother can be happy while her daughter is unhappy shock you? It's the core of the both/and approach, and most of us aren't very good at it. "It's a matter of living with the paradox of opposites and not putting off good feelings until some mythic day in the future when all issues are resolved. When is that

kind of resolution ever going to occur?" asks Anne. "Both/and is acknowledging that two things can be equally true even though they are in opposition—and that they don't cancel each other out. Instead of saying, 'My daughter is unhappy SO I can't stop worrying about it,' you can choose to say, 'My daughter is unhappy AND I'm going to my art class.' Keeping yourself stressed doesn't improve the process of your daughter adjusting to her new school. Your task is not to fix her experience. Your task is to feel joy

while acknowledging things as they are in the here-and-now."

Anne learned about living in the both/and from her own experience. She watched her father decline from a vascular dementia for almost 20 years. "He was diagnosed when he was only 58 years old," she says, "and there was a lot of stress and grief during the slow and profound loss of his health and personality. He was ill while I was in my 30s and 40s, what people often consider the prime of life. Very stressful situations were going on with my dad's health, my mother was struggling to cope, and I was there to support and help. At the same time I also had to stand back and ask myself: *Does this difficult and painful situation define*

everything in my life? Or do I deal with the difficulty and the pain and also choose to live a full, vital, and happy life?"

Because upsetting and unexpected things will always be happening around us, Anne suggests developing the both/and perspective through a three-step process. For example:

1. **Notice what the stressor is: "My father has dementia."**

2. **Acknowledge how you feel about it: "I am sad and angry."**

3. **Choose what to focus on now: "While I visit Dad, I'm connecting with how much I love him."**

This "notice, acknowledge, choose" sequence can be applied to any challenging situation. Joy is not about denial, and it's not the psychological equivalent of putting your fingers in your ears and whistling through the dark. We must notice and acknowledge what's stressing us and consider what options are available, whether we're dealing with a miserable teenager, a parent in declining health, or any other situation that requires us to make decisions on how to best handle the stressor. Once our actions have gone as far as they can go and we've helped the loved one to whatever degree that we can, we are free to choose how we feel. And even in an emotional whirlwind, we can still choose to feel good.

WHEN WAS the LAST TIME YOU FELT TRULY JOYFUL?

If you ask someone what brings her joy, prepare for a significant pause before she answers. Modern humans are so trained to analyze and problem-solve that we can be surprisingly cut off from our personal joy-triggers.

Fortunately, if we take time to get in touch with some of the parts

of ourselves we don't usually notice, we may know more than we think we know. "Your unconscious is aware of what's missing from your life, but we're not taught how to access this knowledge," says Anne. "The unconscious is seen as a dark and murky place and, in a society that's more oriented toward outcome than

process, we don't always trust what it tells us. We need to remember that the unconscious also is the root of creativity and new ideas. If people are willing to 'get out of their heads,' connect with their feelings and intuitions, they often quickly discover what they need and want to bring into their lives."

A meditative practice can help you quietly sit with yourself, giving you the chance to check in and hear that inner voice, and thus experience your intuitive truth. You can also simply notice what feels fun as you go through your everyday life, even if you tend to discount these moments as trivial or wasted time. "We often don't take time to notice the little things we really enjoy or that feel most congruent with our values and sense of self," says Anne. "It's those small moments of awareness that lead to those 'Aha' insights that tell us who we really are."

Many guests who come to Miraval have planned the trip in the wake of some kind of stressful life experience. They've weathered a divorce, the death of a loved one, a job loss, or a medical diagnosis, and are using their visit as time and space to nourish themselves. Relaxation and rest are certainly important. What guests also often find is that the mindfulness focus at Miraval evokes a new level of awareness. Perhaps they thought all they wanted was to feel okay again, but suddenly "okay" doesn't seem like enough. They crave joy, even if they're not entirely sure how to access the feeling. "Many of the people I speak with have trouble even remembering the last time they felt joyful," says Anne, "and they have to think back longer than you might guess to find memories that connect them with their deepest self. Miraval gives them the opportunity to experience joy in the here-and-now and reconnect with who they really are."

THREE ROUTES to JOY
Balance, Resiliency, and Mindfulness

When it comes to tenets of the Miraval philosophy, the trifecta is surely balance, resiliency, and mindfulness. Whether you're talking about physical health, emotional wholeness, healing past trauma, or what it takes to walk across a rope extended 30 feet in the air, it all seems to come down to these three traits. And finding joy is no different.

First of all, balance. If you think of balance as perfect stillness and utter tranquility, it's time to rethink that definition. Because in the real world, balance isn't for sissies; it requires strength and a constant awareness of what's going on both inside of you and around you.

"Balance is active, always in motion," says Anne. "If we think of balance as a static state that is only achieved when all the elements of our lives are in perfect proportion, we will always be disappointed. Living in balance is really about always shifting and adapting with the expected and unexpected happenings in life. I like to use the metaphor of walking the tightrope. The acrobat isn't standing there perfectly still—if he was perfectly still, he would surely fall. Rather, he constantly notices when he is off-balance and constantly returns to center. Finding balance in our daily lives is exactly the same process. Instead of stressing about having a perfectly proportioned life, focus

Loving-Kindness

As a meditation practice, Loving-Kindness can systematically help us to forgive hurts from the past, feel compassion for others, and deepen our level of acceptance for situations beyond our control. Loving-Kindness focuses on four key qualities of love: friendliness, compassion, joy, and calmness. When practiced over time, the meditation expands our focus beyond ourselves and reaches out to extend blessings to those we know and love, those we know and don't love, total strangers, and the world of plants and animals.

The practice begins with extending love and acceptance to yourself. Do you find that surprising? As long as you feel unworthiness or guilt, it's impossible to truly be present for others, so begin by visualizing yourself as if you were a close friend and repeating whatever phrase feels natural to you. It might simply be the words *loving-kindness,* or you might say, "May you have peace. May you have health. May you have joy." You don't have to say the words aloud unless you want to.

From there, let your mind move to someone you love: a spouse or partner, a family member, a friend. Visualize them in as much detail as you can. Reflect on why you love them, the wonderful qualities they bring to your relationship, and then send them the same verbal blessing you sent to yourself in the paragraph above.

Next, expand the circle of your awareness. Bring to mind someone you don't know as well but whom you have positive feelings about: a neighbor or co-worker, a teacher who was helpful to you in the past, or perhaps simply the first face that pops to mind. Repeat the process, wishing this acquaintance peace, health, and joy.

Now it gets a little tricky. Consider someone for whom you don't hold positive feelings. It might be someone you actually know whom you've had conflict with sometime in the past, or perhaps a relative or lover who has hurt you deeply. It might be a politician or public figure whose positions differ from your own. Repeat the process, sending the person loving-kindness as well.

If you struggle at this point, simply skip this step. Loving-Kindness is not about forcing feelings you can't easily access or pretending to be Mother Teresa when you're actually seething inside. You can try blessing this person in later meditations and may feel more accepting then. Loving-Kindness is a practice like any other and changes over time.

Finally, send out blessings with a more global scope. You might imagine the peoples of other nations, your ancestors, grandchildren yet to be born, the animal kingdom, or the world of plants. Expand your awareness as widely as you wish, notice where it settles without judgment, and then send your message of loving-kindness.

Some people find Loving-Kindness an easy type of meditative practice, since it gives them definite phrases or words to repeat, almost like a mantra, and a defined series of steps to go through. Others struggle with it—if they visualize their sister, for example, they may begin to think about what they should get her for her next birthday and become swept up in planning and thinking rather than the meditation. But, as in any other meditation, Loving-Kindness does tend to evolve in practice, so even if you don't automatically access feelings of forgiveness or compassion, don't despair. Try it again at a later date. Over time, many people have found that this systematic blessing of others has become a central part of their spiritual practice.

on cultivating a centering inner foundation that you keep returning to in the midst of life's stresses. It comes down to connecting with what centers and grounds you and continuing to build and nurture that."

Rather than worry about how to achieve balance, your energy is better spent in developing the skills that will help you efficiently sense when you're off balance—because we're all knocked off balance on a daily basis—and quickly make the inner adjustments needed to return to a centered state. As Anne says, "Balance is not the absence of problems or conflicts. Balance does not mean that everything is resolved in life. Balancing is the willingness to make the choices that return us to center over and over and over."

Another component of joy is resilience, a trait the Miraval team experts emphasize as an indispensable characteristic of a healthy life. Resilience is typically thought of as how well we bounce back from stress, illness, and tough times. The question Anne asks is, "What are you bouncing back to? You may be good at bouncing but unless you have something to bounce back to, that center or inner foundation, it feels like flailing or flapping in the breeze. Remember that resilience is also about how we prepare ourselves for those stresses and tough times—the ones we can anticipate as well as the unexpected crises."

In other words, resilience is not just about hopping up from a blow saying, "I'm all right, I'm all right." Exactly like balance, it requires a strong core, a source of strength that we can return to time and time again. And how do we find this strong core? The key, as in so many things at Miraval, is mindfulness. Mindfulness has as many definitions as it has practitioners, but a key element for everyone is the simple question: Where do I put my focus?

Think of mindfulness as a kind of mental flashlight. Whatever we point it on will be illuminated, and what we do not focus on will remain in shadow. For most people, life is busy and complicated, and each day brings us an array of experiences and emotions. Since every event in the day can't carry the same degree of emotional weight in our hearts or demand the same degree of attention in our thoughts, we are constantly sorting through our experiences, prioritizing them, and assigning them a degree of importance in our life. "We make these choices all day long every day," Anne says. "Dozens of things are happening around us and within us, and unconsciously or consciously, we are constantly choosing where to put our focus."

Simply put, if you develop your ability to focus on positive things, you're creating a strong central awareness of what works in your life. Where are the sources of beauty? Who are the friends that make you laugh? What foods or activities make you feel strong and energized? That's why something like a gratitude journal can be a powerful tool. Just as we need to notice and acknowledge our stressors, so too do we need to notice and acknowledge the blessings of each day. Writing down things you are grateful for encourages you to notice all of the good things that are happening in the course of a day and, more specifically, notice what you feel happy about. It's a

"Remember that resilience is also about how we prepare ourselves for those stresses and tough times—the ones we can anticipate as well as the unexpected crises."

way to stay in touch with the both/ and. An unexpected e-mail from an old friend? A beautiful full moon? A favorite song on the radio? A quick hug from your son? These can all provide small but steady drips of positivity that, if noticed and acknowledged, can provide a counterbalance to the inevitable stressors of life.

SOUNDS SIMPLE, SO WHY DON'T WE ALWAYS CHOOSE JOY?

People often struggle with the idea that they can choose their focus or that they have control over how much happiness they experience on a daily basis. They might say, "But of course I can't control my anxiety ... it just comes over me, like a galloping horse dragging me behind it," or "I can't help but worry about . . . ," or "I'm hit with a wave of anger each time I remember . . ."

Anne believes that the idea that we're the helpless victims of our thoughts and emotions is "simply not true. We are able to make choices about how and where we focus; we just haven't learned how. Practices like mindfulness meditation help us become more skilled at observing our thoughts and emotions without becoming swept away by them. Mindfully focusing on and savoring moments that connect us with joy, feeling gratitude in the small blessings of life, is like any other skill—it becomes easier and more natural with awareness and repetition."

You may also want to consider that, on some deeply unconscious level, you might not want to give up your anxieties and depression. "If we're used to feeling fear and worry, they can become our default position," says Anne. "On one level it's miserable, and on another there's something comfortable about it because it's so familiar." It's also possible that stress has been paying off for you in some way. If the whole family knows you get upset to the point of migraines over the thought of hosting the annual Thanksgiving dinner, your sister may volunteer year after year.

Anxiety masquerading as perfectionism or control can also have certain grim payoffs. "Claiming that you won't do anything unless you know you can do it perfectly or unless you know what the result is going to be can keep you in a safe zone," says Anne. "However, that 'comfort zone' also cuts you off from new experiences, pleasant surprises, and growth. You never put yourself in situations where you get to discover anything new or feel the normal discomfort that comes with change, whether it's taking a new job or merely cutting your hair in a different way. People often linger in this state for years, using the excuse of anxiety to keep them from enacting even the smallest changes. What happens, though, is at certain pivotal points in life, the desire for a more authentic and joyful experience finally overwhelms them and forces them to make active choices about how they want to spend the rest of their lives."

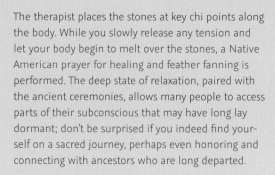

SPA
Sacred Stone Journey

The Sacred Stone Journey is an excellent introduction into Native American spirituality and rituals, as well as a relaxing spa treatment. Guests are escorted by their practitioners to one of Miraval's cozy outdoor spa-treatment huts, where they begin by lying down on a heated massage table. The Sacred Stone Journey employs both hot stones, which are intended to relax and heal the body, and cold stones, which have energizing properties. Used in tandem, the hot and cold stones can bring the body into a state of equilibrium, collectively working to alleviate anxiety, ease aches and pains, boost circulation, and revitalize energy levels.

The therapist places the stones at key chi points along the body. While you slowly release any tension and let your body begin to melt over the stones, a Native American prayer for healing and feather fanning is performed. The deep state of relaxation, paired with the ancient ceremonies, allows many people to access parts of their subconscious that may have long lay dormant; don't be surprised if you indeed find yourself on a sacred journey, perhaps even honoring and connecting with ancestors who are long departed.

The treatment also involves cranial-sacral work. Cranial Sacral Therapy is a gentle, hands-on treatment designed to release tension, relieve pain, and improve your whole body balance. The therapist will very gently cradle your head and points along the spine to release restrictions in the soft tissues that surround the central nervous system.

The Sacred Stone Journey can not only address a wide range of medical problems but can also restore balance throughout the body and bolster your general resistance to both physical illness and stress. This is an excellent treatment for anyone who has recently suffered loss or is struggling with depression or grief.

AT HOME: While the Sacred Stone Journey is exclusive to Miraval, hot stone massages are popular all around the country. To find a practitioner near you, search online or visit a day spa in your hometown.

REINVENTING OURSELVES

A desire for reinvention awakens in many people at midlife. The old ways aren't working anymore. We may have outgrown the choices we made decades ago, or circumstances have changed in ways that make those choices no longer relevant. A pattern that worked early in a marriage may no longer suit a couple that has lived together for 30 years. The job that was once so all-absorbing and exciting suddenly seems to demand too much. The idea of spending the next 30 years like the last 30 creates a panicky flutter in the gut and a new question begins to arise: *Who am I now?*

Some people fight this question for years, either because they fear the answers it could bring or because it seems somehow disrespectful of their present life. If they have financial security, basically good health, and their family around them, they may chastise themselves for wanting more. Midlife reinvention is not a lack of gratitude for what you already have or a desire to repudiate the choices you made years ago. Just because something doesn't suit you now, it doesn't mean it never did or that you're suggesting your spouse/job/spirituality/hometown was a "mistake." You are simply acknowledging that what served you well in a previous stage of your life may no longer work, and that as your life is shifting, so are your priorities. You may have thoroughly enjoyed raising your children and now be just as thoroughly relieved to have them out of the house.

"In midlife we often simultaneously feel the desire to go backward and go forward," says Anne. "Reinventing yourself may actually be a matter of reclaiming your true self without all of the roles and expectations that you've picked up along the way. If you've given up what you loved because you chose to make other things the priority for a while, it's time to revisit those old passions." These interests and activities may take a different form in adulthood—ballroom dance lessons instead of hanging out in the clubs, for example—but anything that once brought you joy might still have the power to move you.

When considering which past passions to revisit, childhood often holds more clues than adolescence. By the time we reached our teens, most of us were acutely aware of how others perceived us and where we fell in the social pecking order. Our desire to fit in may have already begun to pull us away from the core center of what we truly thought and felt. So it may be more helpful to reflect all of the way back to the games you played as a child. Did you love to make up stories? Did you enjoy drawing, swimming, or playing the piano? Did you ride horses, camp out, or pretend to be a spy? These earliest games and fantasies—forged before the world began to press its expectations on us—are sometimes the key to our deepest sources of joy.

In Anne's Mirror of the Soul consultation, participants often find that they've been defining themselves for years by two very limited criteria: the roles they play and their accomplishments. When these things go away or change—sometimes through voluntary life choices like retirement or divorce and sometimes through circumstances we didn't anticipate or want—we can feel lost and even powerless. "The consultation often helps people see that their true center never goes away," says Anne, "no matter what happens to them or how the circumstances of their lives may have changed. You had a core self long before you began assuming the roles you play or racking up those accomplishments. That person is still there."

Just as some people find the answers by looking backward, others choose to go into totally new territory. "Another approach to midlife is to become willing to experiment," says Anne. "Try lots of things and see what you like, what jazzes you, what makes you feel connected to that true self. People often tell me that they want to bring more joy into their life, and then they say, 'I just need to go home and figure it out.' I always call them on that. Our culture teaches we have to 'figure it out' before we begin, that we should know how something is going to end before we can start. The reality is, how are we ever going to know how something will feel until we've begun to experience it? Thinking

"Our discomfort with uncertainty can really hold us back from experiencing new things and discovering what supports us and brings us pleasure."

we have to have it 'figured out' before we begin leaves us in a stuck place."

Perhaps you would like to take a walking tour of Italy but fear you might not be in good enough shape to maintain the pace of the group. Or, you are single and worry everyone else on the tour will be a couple. And, do you need to be able to speak Italian? "Our discomfort with uncertainty can really hold us back from experiencing new things and discovering what supports us and brings us pleasure," says Anne. You can pore over the catalogs and ask people who've been, and you still can't possibly know what a walking tour of Italy will be like for you until you do it. When you're experimenting, you come up against some very basic fears—not just discomfort with uncertainty, but a fear of failure or a dread of looking foolish. And, not all experiments result in what you envisioned. Some things

you try simply won't be a good fit for you. That doesn't mean you've failed. It just means it's time to try something else and see what you discover.

Anne also suggests that you make changes incrementally. "You don't have to turn everything in your life upside down at once," she says. "Gently experiment with new experiences, and be willing to accept a very obvious truth: It's uncomfortable to be outside your comfort zone.

"Discomfort doesn't mean you're doing it wrong," she says. "Discomfort just means you're doing it differently." Reconnecting with joy, even in the face of whatever life throws at you, is so worth it. Joy isn't something that either happens to fall on us or doesn't. It's not a matter of winning the emotional lottery. "Experiencing joy is a choice we make over and over in the midst of the stuff of life."

EXERCISE
Cardio Intervals

Here's the bottom line: An interval workout with steep peaks and low valleys can dramatically improve your level of cardio fitness and dramatically raise your potential to burn fat. Studies at the University of Texas have shown that after a mere two weeks of interval training, the subjects doubled their endurance, while the control group, who exercised without interval training, did not show any measurable improvement in endurance. The interesting thing is that this result held true whether the subjects were very conditioned when they started, completely sedentary, or somewhere in between. Apparently, cardio intervals help everyone, regardless of their fitness level.

At Miraval the Cardio Intervals class moves guests between machines, alternating eight minutes on the elliptical, treadmill, and bicycle. The rotation is designed to keep people from getting bored or risking overuse injuries, but you can easily create your own interval-training program around whatever machine or training regime you have close at hand. The secret, as outlined in detail in the January chapter, is to work at a very high rate during the intervals, pushing yourself right up to the point of exhaustion, and to then recover completely before you begin your next interval.

The real benefit of cardio intervals is not just to improve your cardiovascular fitness levels and burn fat during the workout—although this is clearly a noteworthy benefit in and of itself—but that you're actually training your body to burn more fat during all exercise, even low- or moderate-intensity workouts. So for the sake of your major love muscle—in other words, your heart—as well as your love handles, add cardio intervals to your exercise mix.

KEY POINTS FOR FEBRUARY

✿   While we may fruitlessly search for something or someone to "make us happy," true joy only comes from within.

✿   Situations are rarely totally good or totally bad. By developing "both/and" thinking, we can acknowledge the stressors and challenges in life while still maintaining our ability to feel joy.

✿   If you feel you've lost touch with your heart's true desires, explore the things that brought you pleasure and purpose in the past. It may be time to rekindle a childhood passion.

ANNE PARKER, Wellness Counselor, M.A., M.H.S.A.

Anne has been a professional therapist for more than 30 years, completing degrees in music therapy, counseling psychology, and health-services administration. She brings a unique, practical understanding to creating and enhancing wellness. Anne inspires the discovery of new perspectives about balance, joyful living, and transformation.

Romesco is a rustic, flavorful Spanish sauce based on roasted red peppers, ground raw almonds, and olive oil; and it's surprisingly easy to make from scratch. Our version calls for the addition of crushed tomatoes, sherry vinegar, and bread crumbs for thickening. The result is a sauce that is not only beautifully colored but also wonderfully rich and smoky, and it turns a simple piece of salmon into a hearty winter dish. Heart healthy? Do you even have to ask? The red peppers are high in antioxidants, and salmon provides omega-3 oils, which improve blood flow by preventing platelets from sticking together and thus boost heart health.

MAKES 4 SERVINGS

4 four-ounce wild sockeye salmon fillets (halibut, sea bass, mahi mahi, and snapper are all good substitutes if salmon is unavailable)

1 c. Chimichurri Marinade
(recipe follows)

1 c. Smoky Romesco Sauce

(recipe follows)

1 c. Risotto
(recipe follows)

⅛ tsp. kosher salt

⅛ tsp. freshly ground black pepper

Preheat oven to 425°F.

Place fish in a mixing bowl or casserole dish, and pour the chimichurri marinade over the top. Use a pair of tongs to turn each piece, making sure that each side is coated with the marinade. Place in the refrigerator and marinate for at least 5 minutes or up to 1 hour.

Heat a large ovenproof skillet over medium-high heat. Add the marinated fish and sear for 1 minute.

The excess marinade will serve as the oil needed to sauté. Flip the fish over, transfer the skillet to the oven, and cook for 5 minutes.

Remove the pan from the oven, and let the fish rest in the pan on top of the stove while assembling the romesco sauce.

To plate, spoon ¼ cup of risotto onto each plate, top with a piece of fish, and ladle 2–4 tablespoons of sauce over the top.

MAKES 1 CUP;
SERVING SIZE: 2 TBSP.

½ c. fresh lime juice

½ c. extra-virgin olive oil

½ bunch cilantro, rinsed and drained

½ bunch parsley, rinsed and chopped

1 Tbsp. fresh garlic, minced

Kosher salt to taste

Black pepper to taste

Using a blender or food processor, puree all ingredients together until well blended. Use as a marinade for fish, beef, chicken, or vegetables.

CALORIES: 252; TOTAL FAT: 7 G; CARBOHYDRATES: 19 G; DIETARY FIBER: 1 G; PROTEIN: 22 G

MAKES 4 SERVINGS

SMOKY ROMESCO SAUCE

MAKES 2 CUPS;
SERVING SIZE: ¼ CUP

2 c. red bell peppers, roasted, peeled, and seeded (about 3 medium peppers)

1¾ c. tomatoes, roasted, peeled, and quartered (2 average-sized tomatoes)

¼ c. almonds, raw, blanched, and sliced

1 Tbsp. extra-virgin olive oil

1 Tbsp. sherry vinegar

½ tsp. Spanish smoked paprika

½ tsp. kosher salt

¼ tsp. crushed red pepper or ground dried chipotle chili

1 tsp. garlic, raw, chopped

¼ cup fresh bread crumbs

Combine all ingredients in a blender or food processor and process until smooth, about 30 seconds. Pour into medium sauce pot and simmer for 12 minutes. Adjust seasonings as desired. Remove from heat and serve.

RISOTTO

MAKES 4 SERVINGS

2 cups vegetable stock or canned vegetable broth

¼ tsp. Miraval Oil Blend (3:1 mix of canola oil and extra-virgin olive oil)

1 Tbsp. yellow onion, chopped

¼ tsp. garlic, minced

½ c. arborio or carnaroli rice

½ c. dry white wine

½ tsp. fresh parsley, minced

¼ tsp. fresh oregano, minced

¼ tsp. fresh thyme, minced

¾ tsp. kosher salt

¾ tsp. freshly ground black pepper

1 Tbsp. grated Parmigiano-Reggiano

Place the vegetable stock in a small saucepan and bring to a simmer over medium-high heat. Remove from heat and cover to keep warm until ready to use.

Heat the oil in a medium saucepan over medium-high heat. Add the onion and garlic and cook, stirring until fragrant, about 45 seconds. Add the rice and cook, stirring for 1 minute. Add the wine and cook until reduced by half, 1 to 1½ minutes.

Add 1½ cups of the hot stock and stir well. Cook at a low simmer, stirring occasionally, until nearly all of the stock is absorbed, 6 to 7 minutes. Add the additional ½ cup of stock and cook, stirring occasionally, for 2 minutes. Add the herbs, stir well, and cook for 2 minutes. Add the salt and pepper, stir well, and cook until all of the liquid is absorbed, 1 to 1½ minutes. Add the cheese, stir well, and cook until melted, about 30 seconds.

Remove the pan from heat and serve immediately as an accompaniment for chicken, beef, fish, or vegetarian entrées.

March

MEDITATION If you think of meditation as something you do 20 minutes a day, sitting on a cushion with your legs crossed and your eyes closed, you're only seeing a small part of the many benefits that this ancient practice can bring to your life.

The GENTLE POWER of MEDITATION

[EXPERT] *MaryGrace Naughton*

"MEDITATION ISN'T JUST ABOUT THE CHANGES THAT OCCUR IN YOUR BODY AND MIND DURING THE FEW MINUTES YOU'RE MEDITATING," SAYS MARYGRACE NAUGHTON, YOGA/MEDITATION SUPERVISOR AT MIRAVAL, WHO HAS BEEN PRACTICING MEDITATION SINCE 1987.

"In time, the practice begins to seep into every aspect of your day, bringing greater calm and clarity to all the roles you assume. A regular meditation practice changes your quality of life even when you're not meditating."

While some people meditate as a spiritual practice, others turn to it as a way to alleviate stress and reduce the impact of stress-related illness. When we sit down to meditate, our brain waves gradually shift and we begin to enter a deeper level of consciousness. The mere act of observing our breathing is often enough to help it slow and deepen. This steady breathing leads in turn to muscle relaxation and, eventually, a calmer nervous system. From there the benefits begin to extend to the heart in the form of lower blood pressure and lower cholesterol. The physical benefits of meditation have been so well documented that many doctors consider it a central part of any stress-management package, as essential a component of wellness as exercise, nutrition, and rest.

Since meditation generates a powerful mind-body connection, there are psychological advantages as well as physical ones. Meditation has been proven to help with insomnia, chronic pain, chemical dependency, and post-traumatic stress disorder. It can provide a fresh perspective for people coping with depression and anxiety, since, as MaryGrace says, "Therapy and medication are often designed to 'understand' and 'fix' the problem. Meditation teaches us to observe our mind simply as it is, without judgment or pressure. Sometimes sitting with a feeling like anxiety in a spacious and kind way generates compassion for our experience and can be an effective approach to health and well-being."

Meditation is also linked to higher levels of intuition and creativity and can encourage practitioners to develop qualities such as gratitude, patience, kindness, and empathy. "It helps you to be less reactive," says MaryGrace. "You're not as likely to go through the day with those automatic sort of knee-jerk reactions, saying things like, 'The traffic on the way to work made me crazy,' or 'When she said that, it ruined my whole morning.' Meditation is helpful in establishing a mindfulness practice in day-to-day living. You slow down and choose your response to all these small everyday stressors. And the calmness that results is a type of spiritual practice, even if you didn't enter meditation with that goal in mind."

HOW to BEGIN a MEDITATION PRACTICE

Step one: When beginning to establish a meditation practice, the first step is to forget the notion that there's one magic path that works for everyone. Meditation isn't about doing it right; it's about doing it right for you.

"Meditation can remain challenging, no matter how long you've practiced," says MaryGrace. "There's not a point where you think, *Hooray, I've got it! I'm now a great meditator.* Meditation is an ongoing experience in observing your mind, so a better approach is, *Okay, so this is what my mind is like on this particular day.*" Meditation is an opportunity to observe your body/mind, just as it is, in order to gain freedom from suffering.

Step two: Sit comfortably and naturally. Some people worry that if they slow down for even five minutes, they'll fall asleep. "You might," MaryGrace says, "and, if so, it's no big deal. Maybe you needed the nap. If you want to stay with the practice, rather than sleep, open your eyes and find a single, pointed focus." And if you find yourself falling asleep every time you sit quietly, this could be a sign that you're walking through life exhausted. Look at ways to increase your quality of sleep, which we'll discuss more fully in the October chapter.

Most people find it easier to hold their attention while sitting up. The cross-legged lotus pose associated with statues of the Buddha, and thus meditation, is traditional, but if you find it uncomfortable, it certainly isn't necessary. It helps to keep your spine elongated and straight, both to aid the flow of chi, or life energy, and to avoid back strain but, once again, let comfort be your guide. If you hold yourself too rigidly, you'll have trouble relaxing.

You can opt to close your eyes or perhaps hold them half closed, gazing slightly downward. Your legs can either be crossed if you're on a cushion, or if you're sitting in a chair, relaxed and slightly apart with your feet on the floor. Your shoulders should be even, your chest open, and your hands resting lightly on your knees. Hands can lie either flat down or palms up, and some meditators like to lightly touch their thumbs and first fingers together in an *O* shape to help increase the flow of chi. Your chin should be tucked toward your throat, and it also helps to place the tip of your tongue against your palate near the front teeth.

This might seem like a lot of instructions to "sit naturally and comfortably," but once you get used to it, the position is easy to maintain, even for extended periods of time.

Step three: Don't worry if you can't completely still your thoughts. Despite what you may have been led to believe, an utterly blank mind is not the goal of meditation. "The mind thinks," MaryGrace says, "just like the heart beats and the lungs breathe. It's what they're meant to do." A more realistic goal is to avoid getting pulled into the circular, obsessive thinking some practitioners call "monkey mind." When a thought arises in meditation, simply acknowledge it, and then let it go.

Step four: Finally, create a ritual around your meditation. Find a place in your bedroom, study, or office where you can have privacy and a comfortable chair or cushion. Choose a time when you can most easily retreat for a few minutes. (In some busy households, this may require getting up a half hour before the rest of the family awakens.) And finally, consider how long you can meditate.

"We're creatures of habit, so when we're first establishing a

for the same length of time every session. Consider your lifestyle and be realistic. Maybe on Tuesday you can meditate for 30 minutes, and on Friday you only have five. It's more important to make a commitment before you start that you will sit for a certain time and hold to that commitment than it is to promise yourself you'll meditate the exact same amount of time every day."

Beginners sometimes wonder about how to best time their meditations, especially if they fear they might doze off. It's hard to relax while sneaking occasional peeks at your watch. You can always set your clock or phone to buzz at the end of the time frame you've chosen. There are even phone apps such as the Insight Timer that allow you to select from a menu of pleasant chime notifications to guide you in and out of your session.

A CD of guided meditations can also be helpful; it not only assures you that you'll be led out of the meditation at a specified time, but the leader's voice can both help you relax and bring you back if your mind begins to drift. There's a wide variety of meditation CDs on the market, so you might have to experiment a bit to find the one that's perfect for you. Some are designed to promote general relaxation, while others have a more specific focus, such as physical healing, loving-kindness, or a spiritual journey. The sessions generally range in length from 5 to 45 minutes, but most meditations for beginners last around 15 minutes.

The voice of the leader might also be a factor in your choice; although, you don't want to choose a voice so soothing that it automatically puts you to sleep.

At Miraval, the evening meditations feature different themes for each day, but the morning meditation is always based on Vipassana, or Insight Meditation/Mindfulness, which is described as seeing things as they really are. "Guests often see a stay at Miraval as a way to jump-start their practice," says MaryGrace, "and it is indeed a chance to sample a wide variety of types of meditation and explore which ones attract them. However, since the deepest benefits of meditation are cumulative, their true practice depends on what happens when they go home. There are no shortcuts. Meditating three times a day or going for a 45-minute session instead of one 15-minute session . . . none of that matters as much as consistency and giving it time."

practice, it helps to meditate at the same time every day," MaryGrace says. "For many people, that's either first thing in the morning or immediately after they get home from work. But to get the benefits you don't have to do it every single day, and you don't have to do it

TYPES of MEDITATION

CONCENTRATION MEDITATION

Concentration meditation, where relaxation is achieved by focusing the mind on a particular image, object, or sound, is a good way to start. It can be viewed simply as a way to counteract stress or as the doorway to a spiritual practice.

A classic type of concentration meditation is object practice, where you gaze at something such as a bowl, candle, or flower. Ideally, it's an image that you find attractive and that makes you feel serene. Whatever you select should be placed at eye level so that you aren't straining to look up or down to view it. Then you simply gaze at the object, considering every element of it. You don't have to stare or deliberately focus, and yes, it's permissible to blink.

The purpose of object meditation is to slow the mind and embrace the lost art of close observation. We go through life in a rush, barely listening to conversations and busily striding past things, even lovely things like a flower, with little more than a cursory glance. By helping us see the intricate beauty and individual qualities of a single part of the larger world, object meditation trains us to be more mindful and aware of our surroundings.

Another classic form of concentration practice is sound or mantra meditation. Tibetan bowls create wonderfully round and lingering tones and are popular in meditation groups, as well as being featured in some meditation CDs. Obviously, you can't simultaneously ring the bowls and meditate, but a type of sound meditation you can employ on your own is the repetition of a mantra, where you either chant or silently repeat a specific word or phrase.

"A mantra is a good way to still your mental chatter," says Dr. Jim Nicolai, Medical Director of the Andrew Weil, M.D., Integrative Wellness Program at Miraval. He often combines a mantra with his breathwalking meditation, which was described in the January chapter, using four primordial sounds—Sa Ta Na Ma—synchronized with his breathing. "I like the Tibetan chant," he says, "but it could just as easily be any four-syllable phrase, such as 'Thank you, father' or 'I love my life.' What you say doesn't matter as long as it works for you. The benefit is in using the repetition of sound to still the mind."

Loving-Kindness, described in the February chapter, can also be a form of concentration meditation, albeit a practice with a more direct spiritual and psychological intent. Loving-Kindness meditation is based on a series of prayer-like phrases that can be offered on behalf of the person who is meditating (such as "May I be free from worry"), on behalf of someone else ("May you be well"), or perhaps on behalf of the world ("May all creatures be at peace"). The practice has become extremely popular, with many practitioners reporting that Loving-Kindness has lessened their feelings of anger, anxiety, and sadness.

Whether you prefer gazing at an object, repeating a mantra, or offering a blessing to the world, the key advantage of any form of concentration meditation is that it gives your mind a specific focus and a still place to return when it begins to wander. Many people find this a simpler and less intimidating place to begin than sitting in silence with their own thoughts.

PROGRESSIVE MEDITATION

Progressive meditations are similar to concentration meditations in that they give the mind something to do while meditating. But in a progressive meditation, just as the name implies, there's a systematically guided journey instead of focusing on a still point.

Progressive meditations include chakra meditations, where the attention gradually moves through the seven chakra points in the body, a technique that will be described in detail in the May chapter, and intuitive-guidance meditations, where the practitioner asks for help from a wise figure. When seeking intuitive guidance, the practitioner either frames a question or asks for general insight from Buddha, Jesus, Moses, Mother Mary, or whoever emerges as a spiritual guide. Visualizations, where the meditating person slowly imagines himself or herself going through a specific process, whether it's an Olympic ski run, job interview, or relaxing walk on the beach, is another popular variation. CDs are available to lead you through any of these types of progressive meditation.

Body scans are one of the most helpful types of guided meditation.

Usually the practitioner begins with the sole of the right foot, visualizing an image—it may be the golden warmth of relaxation or a healing white light—moving over each part of the foot and then up the right leg and into the hip. The imagery then flows to the left foot, leg and hip, gradually up the torso and into the arms, and finally to the neck and head. The more slowly and gently you move the intention, the better. For example, you might say to yourself, *The golden glow is washing over the back of my right hand and pooling in my palm. Now it is moving down each of my fingers: thumb, pointer, middle, ring, and pinkie.* Become aware of the sensations in each part of the body—heat, cold, tingling, muscle aches, or tension—without judging them. A body scan is a chance to send unconditional love and gratitude to each part of your body—the legs that carry you through the day, the lungs that give you breath and life, the ears that take in music, and the voices of people you love.

By the time your entire body has been scanned, you're usually in a deep state of calm. For this reason, body scans are good ways to relax before going to sleep each night. They also play a pivotal role in the mind-body connection of healing,

as they help you to "check in" with how each part of your body is feeling at any given time. Sometimes gently directing attention to an area with tension or pain is enough in and of itself to ease that discomfort.

MOVING MEDITATION: YOGA

Yoga and meditation are not the same things, but there are certainly meditative benefits to a yoga practice, and this sort of moving meditation is a good alternative for people who claim, "I'm not the kind to just sit there and meditate."

"Yoga also involves breathing slowly in and out through the nose," says MaryGrace, "and it can thus help calm the mind and the nervous system. But for yoga to give the same spiritual and psychological benefits as meditation, it has to be done with awareness. It's not a competition or a matter of 'Can I wrap my leg around my neck?' Our egos can quickly become engaged in some yoga classes, and our minds start telling us that we should be able to do that perfect pose that the person on the mat beside us is doing. But grasping and straining and pulling are more likely to injure you than help. If done in the right spirit, yoga invites you to listen to

EXERCISE
Energy Yoga

Yoga isn't always mellow. In fact, energy yoga is a butt-kicking, sweat-inducing series of poses that can provide just as many cardio benefits as running or spinning.

Energy yoga engages the Kundalini energy, which gathers at the base of the lower back and then runs up the spine and throughout the body. Students are led through an active flow—a series of cyclic, repetitive movements designed to heat up the body and strengthen the core muscles of the abdomen and back.

And even though you will get hot, you will get a workout, and you will sweat, the ultimate question of energy work is always, "What do you do with it once you have it?" The Miraval Energy Yoga class ends with stillness so that the student can sense the vibrations of the energy he's created and harness this warm, powerful glow for the rest of his day.

the wisdom of your body as well as your mind and can be a wonderful way to gain awareness. Yoga asanas, or postures, were actually developed to help practitioners sit more comfortably in meditation."

As with meditation, there are many types of yoga practices. Miraval offers the following classes. Similar ones may be offered near you.

CORE YOGA develops core strength, especially in the abdomen, and stamina. It includes many balancing poses.

ASHTANGA is a vigorous yoga practice that was developed by Pattabhi Jois and consists of six series of poses synchronized with the breath. Using a full and audible breath (ujjayi), this practice produces internal heat and purifying sweat. Traditionally, a student progresses from one series to the next with the guidance and approval of a certified teacher. The benefits include strength, flexibility, endurance, focus, balance, and purification.

VINYASA is a yoga practice with a broad definition and derives from Ashtanga Yoga. Classes consist of a flowing sequence of postures synchronized with the breath. Classes can vary from vigorous to meditative, depending on the instructor. The benefits include flexibility, focus, balance, and strength.

RESTORATIVE YOGA is a practice that deeply supports the student with an extensive use of props. The practice is one of gentle surrender and deep relaxation, more like being

Yin Yoga

While recent yoga trends have leaned toward the more active, aerobic modalities such as energy or power yoga, there's a place in everyone's practice for calm and stillness. In contrast to the fiery, active, masculine energy of yang, Yin Yoga focuses on the stable, grounded feminine energies.

The motto of Yin Yoga is "let it go." You hold the poses for longer times, allowing the body to slowly stretch. As the muscles begin to lengthen and release, the stretch can go even deeper, involving the ligaments and tendons of the body. The mind is likewise still, making the psychological benefits of Yin Yoga akin to those of meditation.

held in the poses rather than holding the poses. The benefits are relief from chronic stress and tension and a deep state of relaxation of mind and muscles.

DREAM YOGA is a meditative, relaxing class that combines restorative yoga poses with visual components. It is designed to help bridge the gap between the waking and sleep realms and to promote better sleep.

YOGA FLOW links the traditional postures and breath practice of Vinyasa Yoga with more challenging balance postures. Yoga Flow is a quick-paced class that builds both strength and fluidity.

YOGA GROOVES features upbeat contemporary music in the background as students go through the flowing moves of a Vinyasa practice while focusing on the breath.

ENERGY YOGA combines energizing and detoxifying Kundalini moves with Ashtanga-influenced standing postures.

YIN YOGA uses supportive props to help relax the muscles and stretch connective tissues. Yin Yoga is a practice of surrender. Poses are held for extended periods of time, but students are encouraged to listen to their bodies and take breaks as needed.

FLYING DRAGON combines elements of the more flexibility-based yin practice of stretching connective tissues and the more cardio-based yang practice of building strength and "stoking the inner fire." When the yin and yang are in balance, the Flying Dragon practice is a type of "yoga dance" between passive and active moves.

YOGA NIDRA is a meditative practice often referred to as "yogic sleep." The student is guided into a deep state of relaxation while staying awake and aware. The benefits include reduction of stress and deep relaxation and awareness.

Once you become comfortable with object, guided, or yoga-based meditation, you may want to eventually move into the sort of mindfulness meditation that Miraval offers every morning.

VIPASSANA INSIGHT MEDITATION

Buddha proclaimed that the path to enlightenment was mindfulness; vipassana, or mindfulness meditation, evolved from his teachings over 2,500 years ago.

The object of mindfulness is to bring more openness, calmness, and acceptance into our daily lives. It is simply—and not so simply— the practice of observing what is. Mindfulness is about the power of the present moment, using the breath to allow the mind to calm and center itself in the here-and-now. You might use a few deep, conscious breaths to guide yourself into the practice, but beyond that,

vipassana has few rules. You are largely still and silent throughout the meditation.

Simply sitting in silence with your mind free of distractions, even the distraction of a teacher's voice, can be challenging. Thoughts will almost certainly arise, but the object is to observe them, acknowledge them, and then let them move on, like leaves being swept away in a rushing stream. Bodily sensations—the desire to scratch, sneeze, or cough—will likely arise as well. If you want to react to them, that's certainly okay. No one has ever been kicked out of a mindfulness class for scratching their nose. But the deeper challenge is to observe these impulses for what they are. We are often so unaccustomed and thus uncomfortable with stillness and silence that we create little problems like an achy foot to distract us from the potentially terrifying possibility of confronting the void. If you do decide to stretch, scratch, or yawn, just make sure it is a conscious choice to make yourself more comfortable and not merely your mind's attempt to hide behind busywork.

Along with the random thoughts and bodily twinges, which most people expect, may come something else that they don't: strong emotions. But if anger,

sadness, or other feelings arise during vipassana, treat them just like thoughts. You don't need to make a feeling stop or push it down, and the presence of emotion is not the sign you're a bad meditator. Far from it.

Continue to notice what you're feeling, where it manifests in your body, and try to stay present with any emotions that come forth, trusting that whatever arises during vipassana meditation needs to release and be purified. As you become more comfortable simply sitting with thoughts and feelings— greeting them with acceptance instead of a desire to analyze, correct, or change them—you will gradually expand this same awareness into the rest of your life, making you better at observing situations without reacting with rage or depression.

The ability to calmly observe painful events that may be currently happening or that may have happened in our past doesn't mean those things are okay. It doesn't mean we've forfeited the right to respond to unfairness or cruelty when we encounter them. It just means that we have become better at knowing which situations we can change and which we can't, and thus mindfully choosing what our reactions will be.

BAKED APPLE TORTELLI

Why a dessert for the meditation chapter? A dessert is the perfect chance to practice mindful eating, which requires us to slow down and appreciate our food. Savor each bite, noting not only the varieties of taste but also variations in texture: the smoothness of a cream filling, the flakiness of crust, the crunch of an apple.

Speaking of apples, the Baked Apple Tortelli below is warm and satisfying, a light variation on a classic homey dessert. The apples, pears, and raisins encased in a crisp outer shell give it the feel of a fruit turnover, while the unusual mix of spices lift it to a new level of sophistication. Ginger, clove, and aniseed? Grandma's apple pie was never quite like this.

MAKES 12 SERVINGS

2 Tbsp. orange juice

½ vanilla bean, cut in half horizontally and seeds scraped out

1 apple, peeled, cored, and diced

1 pear, peeled, cored, and diced

¼ c. pineapple, diced

1 tsp. raisins

1 tsp. mixed orange and lemon zest

½ tsp. fresh ginger, minced

Pinch of clove

Pinch of aniseed

Pinch of cinnamon

FOR THE DOUGH

⅓ c. evaporated raw cane sugar

6 Tbsp. low-fat cream cheese

1 large egg

2 large egg whites

1 tsp. baking soda

¼ c. fat-free milk

2½ c. unbleached flour

FOR ASSEMBLY

1 large egg, lightly beaten

Powdered sugar

FILLING In a large sauté pan, heat the orange juice and vanilla bean and seeds to a low boil. Add the remaining ingredients, and sauté until the apples and pears are tender, approximately 15 minutes. Refrigerate until chilled.

DOUGH Beat the sugar and cream cheese until soft. Slowly add in egg and egg whites, scraping down the sides of the bowl after each addition. Dissolve the baking soda in warm milk. Place flour in a large bowl or on a cutting board. Make a well in the center of the flour and place egg mixture and milk into the center. Stir the center ingredients with a fork, and then begin drawing the flour, starting with the inside walls of the well, into the center until all of the flour has been incorporated. The dough will form into a moist rough ball.

Lightly flour a work surface and roll out the dough to ⅛ inch thickness. Cut out 3-inch circles and place 1 teaspoon of the filling onto the center of each circle. Fold the circles in half and seal edges with the tines of a fork. Place tortelli on a baking sheet lined with parchment and sprayed with a nonstick spray. Brush each tortelli with the lightly beaten egg and bake at 350°F for 15 to 20 minutes or until golden brown. Cool and dust with powdered sugar.

CALORIES: 200; TOTAL FAT: 46 G; CARBOHYDRATES: 35 G; DIETARY FIBER: 1 G; PROTEIN: 6 G

WELL

April

WELLNESS Over the last few decades our cultural definition of health has slowly begun to expand. While our grandparents probably thought of health as the absence of a serious disease, the modern generation is setting the bar much higher. We want more than to be merely "not sick." We want optimal wellness—a state of energy and balance, of being the best we can be—and we're demanding a set of tools that will allow us to extend this wellness deep into our senior years.

OPTIMAL WELLNESS

[EXPERT] *Jim Nicolai, M.D.*

UNFORTUNATELY, SOME MEMBERS OF THE MEDICAL PROFESSION HAVEN'T YET CAUGHT UP WITH THE INCREASED EXPECTATIONS OF THEIR PATIENTS. AND EVEN IF YOUR DOCTOR IS SYMPATHETIC TO YOUR NEEDS, HE MAY BE HAMSTRUNG BY THE TIME CONSTRAINTS OF HIS PRACTICE.

As a result, the typical annual physical goes something like this: During the examination, your doctor is systematically going through a checklist of possibilities, trying to make sure nothing on that list is wrong with you in a physical sense. He's looking for diseases that are measureable, specific, and easy to confirm through tests and procedures. If he doesn't find any of these problems, you're pronounced "normal." If he does find something, he'll introduce strategies—most likely pharmaceutical or surgical ones—to either eradicate the disease, or if that's not possible, at least keep it under control. When and if these strategies work, you'll be pronounced "cured," "stabilized," "medically managed," or "in remission."

What you probably won't be called is "healthy." The world of medicine spends a lot of time thinking about disease and virtually none thinking about health.

This black-and-white thinking —you're either sick or you're not— ignores the deeper truth, which is that wellness exists on a spectrum. It's quite possible for people to be free from serious illness but still not come anywhere close to reaching their optimal levels of health. They don't have enough energy to get through their day; they don't sleep well; they seem to catch every bug that's running through the office; and it takes them weeks to shake off these little setbacks. They aren't necessarily feeling horrible, but neither are they feeling great. They're existing in a state of subpar wellness and thus not reaping the best that life has to offer.

Wellness is often associated with wholeness, which means that it requires looking at health through a broader lens. If a patient shows up in a doctor's office and is diagnosed with diabetes or celiac disease, the doctor will most likely prescribe medication and make suggestions about dietary changes. But it's highly unlikely he'll ask the patient about her sleeping patterns, her relationships, or how well she's performing at work. It sounds almost ridiculous to suggest it: "Your blood-sugar levels are high. Are you getting along with your husband?"

Yet both celiac disease and diabetes—along with a large number of other ailments ranging from sleep apnea to kidney disease—have been linked to a higher incidence of depression. The causality works both ways; dealing with chronic disease can make a person anxious or depressed, and in turn, anxiety and depression can put a person at a higher risk for disease. All of the parts of our lives are interconnected. We don't get sick in pieces, even if it sometimes seems that we do. Therefore, we don't get well in pieces either.

"If we look closely at the word *disease*, it breaks into *dis-ease*," says Jim Nicolai, M.D., the Medical Director of the Andrew Weil, M.D., Integrative Wellness Program at Miraval. "And so the deeper definition focuses on anything that cuts into our sense of ease or well-being.

Health isn't just the ability to drag through the day—it's wholeness, balance, and resilience. But reaching that state requires a set of tools that are specific to each individual. Most doctors aren't trained to ask these broader questions, or even if they do understand the mind-body-spirit connection, they often don't have the time to sit with each patient and say, 'You're not sick, but let's talk about how we can we make you feel even better.' They're geared to put out the fire right in front of them and then move on to the next. If we as individuals expect to reach optimal wellness, we certainly want to look for the best possible medical guidance, but we also have to realize that we're ultimately responsible for our own health."

TRUSTING OUR BODY'S ABILITY to HEAL ITSELF

The language of modern health care illustrates that, as a culture, we see illness as something we must vigorously fight. We speak of the "battle against breast cancer" or "warding off a cold." There are indeed times when we must take strong aggressive action against a disease, but on a day-to-day basis, Dr. Jim says, "our bodies are remarkably adept at healing themselves. The problem is we often don't pay attention to our bodies at all until they malfunction in some way, and then we become hypervigilant. So, we're much better at recognizing, analyzing, and describing sickness than health. If you turn your attention to realizing what foods, activities, and situations make you feel great, you can make a conscious decision to bring more of them into your life. In the long run, it's more effective to nurture what's good than to try and defeat what's bad."

An overreliance on modern medicine, especially in the form of prescription drugs, has shaken our collective faith that our bodies have the natural ability to self-regulate and self-heal. As Dr. Jim suggests, we're very much like the doctors we may complain about—obsessing over the small complaint and ignoring the bigger picture. We're more likely to notice which foods give us acid reflux than we are to notice which foods make us feel energized. We complain about the night of insomnia but don't bother to analyze what conditions existed the next night, when we slept well. And we're so focused on the muscle we strained playing tennis that we don't stop to consider how much better we've felt overall since we started to exercise.

"Wellness requires us to adjust our thinking," says Dr. Jim, "from what isn't working to what's going great. You probably already know what makes you sick, but have you stopped to consider what makes you well? Expanding and exploiting what works is the best way to prevent illness and to recover quickly from any diseases we do have."

Along with good choices about our diet, exercise, and rest, optimal wellness also requires us to look at

SPA
Grounding Facial

Your skin is the only thing protecting you from the outside world—keeping vital elements like moisture in and undesirable elements like pollution out. It's the body's largest organ, and nothing reflects your wellness—mental and physical—quite like the condition of your skin.

The Grounding Facial, a Miraval exclusive developed by Clarins, is a 70-minute journey into the world of plants, using 100 percent pure botanical extracts to deepen relaxation, ease fatigue, and shift you to a place of well-being. The facial begins with the placement of warm stones onto your skin to help relax facial tension and open the pores. Then, a botanical double cleanse dislodges embedded makeup and impurities, followed by a mood-lifting facial massage and a hydrating mask.

AT HOME: A facial is one of the easiest spa treatments to re-create at home. Just follow these steps. 1) Start with an attitude adjustment. Light a candle. Put up your hair. Turn on soft music. Remove all your makeup and prepare to tune out. 2) Place a small amount of a gentle exfoliating cleaner onto your fingertips, and gently massage into your damp skin until it forms a lather. Exfoliate all around your face, avoiding eye contours. Rinse well with warm water, and then pat dry with a cotton towel. 3) Apply a mask such as the Clarins Beauty Flash Balm, which uses an olive-tree extract to smooth the skin's surface and eliminate signs of fatigue. Leave it on for 5 to 10 minutes, perhaps while you do a brief guided meditation, and then rinse and pat dry. 4) Rebalance your skin with face treatment oil, choosing one made of pure plant extracts. Put a few drops of the oil on a steamed washcloth and then place on your face, slowly breathing in the aromatic essences. Not only does the warmth of the washcloth aid in the absorption of the oils, but it also helps you to relax.

how we handle stress. Most people are aware that stress can make them sick, but what they may not know is that stress keeps us sick by undermining our natural resiliency. Biochemicals released from the brain during various mood states affect how well our body heals itself, and stress hormones such as cortisol and epinephrine can actually make our immune system less responsive. Meanwhile, "feel good" neurotransmitters such as dopamine and hormones like oxytocin help us recover faster and better.

"It's one thing to say that our bodies are designed to heal themselves; unfortunately, we have to also factor in that modern life has done a lot to gum up the works," says Dr. Jim. "If you have a sedentary lifestyle, eat an overprocessed diet with virtually no whole foods, and get little quality sleep, you're weakening the body's natural defenses and making yourself increasingly vulnerable to a wide range of illnesses. Then when you add stress, especially chronic everyday stressors, to the mix you're practically opening the door and inviting disease to come in, pull up a chair, and stay awhile."

LIFESTYLE IS the NEW PILL

The good news is that whenever lifestyle has caused or helped contribute to a disease, it can also be the solution. "Lifestyle is the new pill," says Dr. Jim. "If bad choices got you to a certain physical place, good choices are the way to get you back out of it."

Dr. Jim estimates that a whopping 70 to 90 percent of the diseases he sees in his practice have a lifestyle component and that in the majority of those cases, stress—usually taking the form of anxiety, depression, or insomnia—is the major culprit. "Over the last hundred years, medicine has done a good job treating infectious diseases such as smallpox, polio, and tuberculosis," says Dr. Jim. "Most of the things that killed our great-grandparents just aren't killing people today. And more recently, we've made significant strides in the treatment of injury and trauma. Now the new frontier is treating chronic illnesses like heart disease, which are largely lifestyle based and aggravated by stress."

With this in mind, the new "prescription" might come in the form of wellness recommendations: changes in diet and exercise, dietary supplements, and stress-management techniques. "The big payoff is that a pill only targets a specific condition, but lifestyle choices protect us from a wide range of possible diseases and solve a wide range of problems," says Dr. Jim. "If you can use exercise and meditation to get your stress under control, you will not only lower your blood pressure but also experience better sleep and digestion. This is whole-person medicine."

Of course, these potential turnarounds are based on the assumption that people are willing to change their lifestyles, while a quick glance around your office or neighborhood—or even into your mirror—proves that's not always the case. Revamping your food habits or starting an exercise program is hard work, and even something like beginning a meditation practice requires a commitment of time and focus. The road to lifestyle-based disease is paved with good intentions. Of course, we know all of the things we need to do. But we tell ourselves we'll do them next year, when we have more time.

In addition, on a subconscious level some people like their disease. You may know a person who talks about her ailments all of the time, as if her health, or the lack of it, is the basis of her identity. Illness has become a handy excuse not to do things she didn't really want to do anyway. People are sometimes heavily invested in seeing their particular condition as something that just happened to them—either plain bad luck or some sort of genetic curse. As a result, the last thing they want to hear is that they've brought it on themselves through a series of bad lifestyle choices.

"If the doctor starts talking to a patient about what they've been eating or how much they drink," says Dr. Jim, "the patient sometimes reacts as if the doctor is blaming him. And if a patient thinks the doctor is saying that a disease is all his fault, it's over. The trust is broken, and he's going to resist anything the doctor says after that. So, we have to turn the attitudes around before we can start to change the behaviors. Many people have been telling themselves a story for years, something like, 'Diabetes runs in my family so I can't do anything about it.' If they change their story, they can start to change their condition, but first they have to buy into the idea that change is possible. Yes, they might have a genetic predisposition toward certain diseases, but their lifestyle choices have a huge impact on their health, often trumping that genetic tendency."

WHAT A PERFECT WELLNESS PLAN LOOKS LIKE

A wellness consult at Miraval is simultaneously state of the art and old-fashioned. State of the art in the sense it takes advantage of a wide range of both conventional and alternative modalities and old-fashioned in the sense it is based on a trusting relationship between the doctor and patient.

In bygone days, people knew their family doctors well, and the doctor may well have treated the patient throughout his whole life. "In the modern medical model, we've lost this sense of friendship and continuity," says Dr. Jim. "Not only might you see a different doctor in the practice each time you visit, but the schedule probably allocates a very limited amount of time, like 15 minutes per patient. That's one of the reasons doctors like to become familiar with a single type of medication and write the same prescription for everyone. Modern medicine, in fact, is built around the assumption that in the interest of time efficiency, you should treat every patient more or less the same way."

Dr. Jim gives the example of vitamin D deficiency, something that's so common in America that estimates range from 30 to 60 percent of the overall population. But since there's debate in medical circles about what constitutes a proper blood level of vitamin D and appropriate dosages for supplements, it's an issue many doctors let slide. Probably most of the people reading this have never discussed vitamin D with their doctors at all.

"If your vitamin D levels aren't optimal," Dr. Jim says, "this can affect everything from your bone density to your ability to lose weight. Americans have become much more conscious of sun damage in the last two decades, and our increased use of sunscreen has done good things for the rate of skin cancer. But on the flip side, the fact that we're avoiding even moderate amounts of sun exposure has made it harder for us to keep our vitamin D levels where they should be. If the patient is borderline or deficient, the doctor should sit them down and discuss diet and supplements, keeping in mind that the same dose doesn't work for everyone. But because this issue is individualized and it's time-consuming to figure out where a specific patient is on the vitamin D scale and what to do about it, this is a good example of the kind of conversation that often doesn't happen."

When a guest books a session at Miraval, Dr. Jim and the wellness team review her overall health history and current lifestyle situation. The program is built around Dr. Andrew Weil's premise that health is "a positive sense of wholeness and balance along with the resilience to function effectively in one's environment without being hurt by any of the potentially harmful influences they encounter." But before you can help someone function more effectively in that environment, you have to know what that environment is, so the evaluation protocol includes not only the questions you might

> "My goal is for the guest to leave with an honest understanding of which lifestyle issues are either presently affecting her health or could cause problems in the future . . ."

expect—such as medical problems, medications, surgeries, and family history—but also contains questions designed to gain a broader picture of the patient's life.

"Since our goal is to treat a whole person and not just a shoulder or gall bladder," says Dr. Jim, "in our initial evaluation, we're looking at where the patient is mentally, emotionally, spiritually, and socially as well as physically. No medical test can tell you all these things; you have to pull up a chair and sit and talk. So we ask a lot of questions, trying to zero in on the specific challenges and stressors of a person's daily life. If she's recently moved away from her family and old friends, has a job that requires a lot of travel, or is up three times a night with a newborn, of course any of these situations is going to impact her stress levels and overall quality of life. So we need to know these things just as much as we need to know her cholesterol level. Collectively, these questions allow us to get a more holistic picture of what a guest's health really looks

like, and they also have an impact on the wellness program we create for her. In order to really work, a wellness program needs to be individualized and nuanced. It's easy to say a person should get more whole foods and whole grains into her diet, but if she travels every week for work and eats the majority of her meals in restaurants, that has to be factored in. This person is going to need specific advice about what to look for on menus and what constitutes a good snack for the road."

The guest also produces a personal inventory, ranking how they feel they're doing in various categories of their life on a scale of one to ten, with one being the worst and ten being the best. "Two specific areas can give me a lot of information in a very short time," Dr. Jim says. "How a person evaluates their energy/vitality levels and how they rate their stress. If someone gives herself a three in energy/vitality and a ten in stress, it's pretty clear where to start."

The guest must also be fully on board with the wellness plan and

willing to admit the places where their self-care is falling short. Dr. Jim says some Miraval guests react "with shock" when they realize they're about to sit down and actually talk to a physician for 90 minutes about all of the aspects of their life. In a typical medical setting, the doctor might turn with his hand on the door as he's leaving the office and ask something like, "How are you sleeping?" and the patient may say, "Fine," or perhaps gloss over her sleep difficulties with a joke. She may later complain that the doctor didn't give her enough time, but on another level she may be relieved that he didn't mention issues like her smoking or recent weight gain, or that if he addressed them, it was with a slight slap on the wrist.

It's harder to gloss over problems in a full consult. Issues emerge in an extended conversation that might otherwise never come to light and thus become part of the treatment plan.

"My goal is for the guest to leave with an honest understanding of which lifestyle issues are either presently affecting her health or could cause problems in the future," says Dr. Jim. "And she is also armed with a realistic plan of action that might include stress-management strategies to employ, vitamins and nutritional supplements to take, and changes in diet and exercises." Since Miraval guests are surrounded by a circle of lifestyle modification experts, Dr. Jim frequently refers them to a nutritionist, personal trainer, or wellness counselor as part of their overall treatment regimen. He might also suggest therapies available at the spa, such as acupuncture, Cranial Sacral Therapy, or some form of therapeutic massage.

"We're lucky here, because there's a wealth of options," he says. "I can direct them toward one of our challenge activities, to a yoga or Chi Gong class, or to work with one of our trainers on an exercise plan or even something as specific as improving their posture. We have amazing practitioners who are brilliant at offering life-changing experiences to the guest who is in need of a shift in perspective or an alternate approach to their health conditions."

The plan includes the opportunity to follow up with these experts once the guest goes home. "Lifestyle changes don't occur overnight," says Dr. Jim, "so we're looking to create an ongoing relationship with guests. A trusting partnership means that when they leave Miraval, we can continue the momentum we've created. We keep in touch via e-mail and telephone so that we can discuss the issues that arise when they are trying to implement their program back home. Our goal is to maintain the experience we've established and to keep encouraging, educating, and motivating guests as they implement and even move beyond those initial suggestions."

ASSEMBLING YOUR WELLNESS TEAM

Of course, not everyone is at Miraval, and implementing a lifestyle plan at home is a little more challenging, especially if you live in a small town where all of the resources you need might not be readily available. Your first impulse might be to designate your doctor as your wellness coordinator, but this isn't always practical either. He or she may not have the expertise to suggest and coordinate alternative therapies, even those as mainstream as nutrition counseling, and as we've discussed, your medical visits may already be perfunctory and rushed.

You'll probably need to assemble your own wellness team. It might include your medical doctor, a nurse practitioner, a physician's assistant, a nutritionist, a personal trainer, and a bodywork therapist. "If you have ten minutes a year with your M.D.," Dr. Jim says, "it probably makes more sense to discuss your menopausal symptoms or any problems you're having with your weight-loss program with the nurse practitioner or physician's assistant. The odds are they can give you a lot more time and attention."

As for the more "out there" members of the team, you may have to do research online to find good therapists in various modalities, but once you do, your M.D. may not be as resistant to their suggestions as you might think. "There was a time not too long ago when traditional medicine and alternative medicine were very suspicious of each other," Dr. Jim says. "An M.D. would never have suggested massage or acupuncture to a patient, and alternative practitioners looked on conventional treatments such as drugs or surgery as uniformly bad. But the so-called dinosaurs are finally dying out, and in modern health care both sides are more open to collaborating on solutions that work."

Dr. Jim believes these integrative approaches are the future of medicine. "I've seen orthopedic surgeons work hand in hand with chiropractors, massage therapists, and acupuncturists," he says. "A new generation of doctors is being trained to offer people this sort of guidance. We're seeing medicine change in a powerful way, one doctor at a time."

But regardless of how receptive your doctor is to integrative practices or how great a team you manage to assemble, the captain of that team should be the person who cares the most—in other words, *you*.

"No one else has as much at stake, and no one else knows exactly how you feel," says Dr. Jim. "People need to take charge of their health care, do research, ask questions, and be willing to experiment with different solutions. The acupuncture that helped your friend with back pain might not be as successful with you. But if you keep looking, you may find something that is."

"A new generation of doctors is being trained to offer people this sort of guidance. We're seeing medicine change in a powerful way, one doctor at a time."

REEVALUATING PRIORITIES

Initiating a wellness program isn't just time consuming for medical professionals. The person who really has to commit time, energy, and money to the change is the patient. But what makes someone who's been plodding along with "good enough" health care decide to make these changes and to persist even when their plans hit the inevitable setbacks, plateaus, and snags?

Many of the people Dr. Jim sees at Miraval have had a significant event that shook them up, some sort of "Aha" moment. "Maybe a man has known for years he needs

to stop smoking and clean up his diet," says Dr. Jim. "And then suddenly his next-door neighbor drops dead while mowing the lawn. He thinks, *That could have been me*, and it scares the living daylights out of him. He shows up saying, 'Doc, just tell me what I need to do.'"

This sort of near miss might be enough to drive someone to their doctor's office, or even to a health spa like Miraval, but it isn't always enough to prompt a real change. "Fear can be a strong short-term motivator, but it doesn't last," says Dr. Jim. "A man sitting in an intensive-care unit hooked up to machines might vow to come off the cigarettes, but six months later, when he's in a smoky bar watching football with his friends, that fear is forgotten. It can be so easy to light up."

The people who make changes that last have usually been moved on a much more profound level, what Dr. Jim calls "shaken to the core." Their motivation is not merely a health scare but a genuine desire to build a different and better life.

"The people who really reinvent themselves haven't just been knocked down," says Dr. Jim. "They've been taken to a whole new

place. They don't show up saying, 'How do I get back to where I was?' They show up saying, 'Everything in my life is changing, and I don't know how to handle it all. Can you help me get through it?'"

These people often see Miraval as an oasis, an escape where they can temporarily disconnect from the distractions of their day-to-day life. "The resort is a safe place to step out of your comfort zone with the understanding that getting out of your comfort zone is, by definition, uncomfortable," says Dr. Jim. "But here you have the perfect setting and plenty of support to experiment in moving past your previous limits and process the changes you've been through. It's okay to get scared or sad, because we have so many people around to support you through those healthy emotions. By having new types of experiences in a controlled environment, maybe you'll begin to see where you're stuck back home and start to ask yourself, *How can I do life in a different way?* A retreat like Miraval is much more than a place to get a great massage. It's the perfect setting to question who you think you are."

Healing Visualization

Most healing visualizations begin with establishing a sense of ease within the body. Sit or lie comfortably, making sure the temperature of the room is pleasant and your clothing is not restrictive. You will probably be directed to take a few slow, calming breaths, and you may be asked to picture yourself in a beautiful place—perhaps a meadow, beach, or forest. The acts of closing your eyes, breathing deeply, cuing in to your guide's voice, and journeying to your personal happy place can begin to shift your brain waves from an alert "thinking and doing" state into a calm "listening and responding" state.

The progressive part of the meditation can take many forms. You may imagine a healing light moving through your body or envision the colors of the chakras. For others, it takes the form of a surge of energy, perhaps by visualizing energy moving up from the earth into your body. Some meditations suggest that you systematically tense and then relax each part of the body—clinching your fingers, for example, and holding the tension until you're

instructed to release it with a deep, cleansing breath, and then moving on to tense and relax your arms. Most visualizations scan the entire body, but you can certainly opt to direct your focus to a certain spot—the torn rotator cuff or the arthritis in your hand—and send the wounded places an extra dose of warmth and energy.

Whatever form the visualization takes, the goal is to leave your body relaxed, receptive, and open to healing. As with all kinds of meditation, regular practice is a good way to alleviate general stress, lower your blood pressure, and boost your immunity. But healing visualization, not surprisingly, is especially effective for people who are facing trauma or illness. Medical research has shown healing visualization to be beneficial in reducing pain in hospital patients, especially children, and for lowering the anxiety levels of women in labor. It has also proven especially effective for cancer patients who are undergoing challenging treatments such as chemotherapy and radiation.

RESILIENCE

There's one other component in the issue of optimal wellness, and it may be the most important one of all—*resilience*.

You might go home from Miraval fired up to start the world's most ideal wellness program. You may eat an organic, anti-inflammatory, whole-grains

diet; implement a balanced exercise plan; meditate three times a day; take the right amounts of the right supplements . . . and still get sick. Because life happens. Wellness strategies can certainly reduce the chances you'll get certain illnesses, but no program is bulletproof. Sooner or later, some area of your

life will get out of whack, and believe it or not, that's where the true benefits of wellness kick in.

"Life is going to throw all kinds of stuff at you," says Dr. Jim. "That's inevitable. It may come in the form of something physical, like a disease or accident, or it might come in the form of mental, emotional, or

Chi Gong EXERCISE

Chi Gong, also known as Qigong, is a series of simple but profound movements that have been used in China for more than 4,000 years to strengthen the energy system. The practice helps you gain balance and flexibility, and studies indicate Chi Gong can also drop stress levels, increase the strength of your immune system, and regulate hormonal function, especially in women.

Some people find that focusing on the subtle and fluid movements of a Chi Gong sequence is a more suitable form of meditation for them than sitting on a cushion. The martial art Tai Chi stemmed from the roots of Chi Gong, and both practices involve synchronizing breath and movement, and thus moving through a series of postures with mindful intention.

Movements such as "pushing hands" may look simple but have the power to awaken vital energy centers within the body, increasing the chi or life force. The movements are repetitive and easy to learn but can have a profound impact on health and vitality. Different postures are linked to the stimulation and purification of specific bodily organs, making Chi Gong especially helpful for women going through menopause, anyone who is in rehab or suffering post-operative pain, those with sleep disorders, and older people who are concerned with maintaining and improving their balance.

spiritual pain. The question is 'How well do you get back up?' People who are functioning at an optimal level of wellness can experience an infection or stress or have the emotional heartbreak of losing someone they love, but they'll also have the ability to recover faster and with less lasting damage. They're like those children's toys called Weebles. You can knock them down. You can even hold them down, but the second you let go, they spring right back. That's the kind of health you want to have."

And of course there's one physical challenge that comes to everyone eventually, which is aging. "People who make smart lifestyle choices can certainly hold many

diseases at bay longer than those who don't," says Dr. Jim. "But the real payoff is that when and if they do develop certain ailments, they recover faster and get right back to their lives. We see studies that talk about a certain medicine or treatment adding years to a patient's life, but the real question is 'What was the quality of those years?' Wellness isn't just about increasing our numerical life span but increasing the quality of how we feel as we age."

This is the idea behind a term Dr. Weil has popularized, "The Compression of Morbidity." The endgame of wellness strategies is to separate the onset of age-related disease from the actual aging process for as long as possible. We may

think of aging as a slow incremental slide into the inevitable, but when morbidity is compressed, people lead well and active lives until weeks or even days before their death, with a rapid drop-off at the end. Thus, the pain and suffering is shortened, and the amount of time spent in vigorous health is lengthened. This isn't just a good thing for the individuals who are spared years of misery with a chronic illness, but it also spares society the cost of keeping a whole generation in nursing homes and hospitals for decades. "Living longer is pointless unless we know how to live better," says Dr. Jim. "The goal of wellness is to keep life enjoyable to the very end."

The ATTITUDE THAT LEADS to "SPONTANEOUS HEALING"

In his workshops at Miraval, Dr. Jim discusses the issue of "spontaneous healing" and the fact that while some people crumble under daily stressors, others seem to have an amazing ability to bounce back from adversity on every level. Through working with many patients, he believes that the people who survive serious health issues have the following traits in common.

They're passionate: They love life and they're willing to engage with it.

They're responsible: Rather than abdicating control of their lives to other people, including doctors and therapists, they realize that they have options and that much of the quality of their life is within their control. They seek advice and implement it when appropriate, but they realize the most important decisions should be made from within.

And finally, they're what Dr. Jim calls, "a weird combination of open-minded and stubborn. If there's a problem, they'll keep looking for the solution, trying different things until they find it. They're not stuck in the idea that only one type of treatment or one type of doctor can save them. If the first thing they try doesn't work, they don't just throw in the towel. *They persist.* They believe that it's always possible to get better."

KEY POINTS FOR APRIL

✻ Optimal health is more than just the absence of disease. It is a state of being fully alive and energetic, "the best that we can be." Wellness is the feeling we get when we use our tools to move us toward health.

✻ Lifestyle is the new pill. If certain choices in our diet, exercise, rest, and stress-reduction regimes have brought us into a state of dis-ease, better choices can bring us back out.

✻ Attaining optimal health may require you to assemble a team of professionals—not just your medical doctor, but perhaps a dietitian, exercise physiologist, massage therapist, and energy healer as well.

JIM NICOLAI, M.D.

Jim is the Medical Director of the Andrew Weil, M.D., Integrative Wellness Program at Miraval. He is a board-certified family practitioner and graduate of the Integrative Medicine Fellowship at the University of Arizona in Tucson, under the direction of Dr. Andrew Weil.

Dr. Jim has a special interest in whole-person medicine. His expertise is in combining conventional medicine with the intelligent use of complementary and alternative therapies, including herbs and other botanicals, vitamins, supplements, lifestyle management, and stress reduction. Dr. Jim is the author of Integrative Wellness Rules, *published by Hay House.*

FRUIT ENERGIZER SMOOTHIE

Spring has sprung, and it's time to get outside and explore the natural world. With all this exercise and movement, we need snacks that will give us energy without slowing us down, and nothing is as refreshing or as slam-dunk delicious as this mango-peach smoothie. "Freeze the mango and the peach a little before you put them in the blender," advises Miraval Chef Justin Macy. "That way the texture of the smoothie is thick and perfect."

This is the thinking girl's smoothie—a snap to make but packed with antioxidants such as vitamins A and C. The addition of tart grapefruit juice helps you to avoid the too-sweet stickiness of apple or orange juice, and the aromatic tarragon is the perfect complement to the tropical flavors. And with only six words of instruction and four ingredients to keep on hand . . . hey, how simple is that?

MAKES 1 SERVING

2 c. frozen mango chunks, partially thawed

1 c. frozen sliced peaches, partially thawed

½ c. grapefruit juice

1 Tbsp. tarragon

Combine all ingredients and blend well.

CALORIES: 100; TOTAL FAT: 0.5 G; CARBOHYDRATES: 25 G; DIETARY FIBER: 3 G; PROTEIN: 2 G

May

NUTRITION The old food pyramid has been toppled, replaced with new dietary priorities and a new attitude. The buzzwords may be *color-spectrum eating* and *anti-inflammatory diet*, but the advice boils down to this: If it makes you feel good, eat it.

Our bodies know what they need, and if we pay attention to their signals of satiety and hunger and offer them a variety of fresh, natural, plant-based options, they will gravitate to the right nutritional choices. This isn't about a diet or food deprivation; it's about food exploration.

stress response can save our life when there's a genuine reason for it—it's appropriate for our heart rate to rise and our breathing to quicken in a true crisis. But when stress becomes our status quo state for daily living, a life-saving response can become life-threatening. Likewise, when inflammation exists on a cellular level all over the body, it's a natural defense run amok, and chronic inflammation may be linked to a host of ailments: certain kinds of cancer, heart disease, Parkinson's disease, autoimmune disorders, type II diabetes, and even age-related memory loss.

Fortunately, diet can play a big role in the reduction of chronic inflammation. The anti-inflammatory diet is based primarily on fruits and vegetables, whole grains, and beans and legumes, as well as healthy fats such as olive oil, canola oil, nuts, and seeds. Fish and seafood are important, especially if you choose oily, cold-water fish caught in the wild like Alaskan salmon, black cod, or sardines. Herbs, spices, and green tea are included, as are heart-healthy treats such as a glass of red wine a day and occasional small amounts of dark chocolate. "I'd be happy if people found a way to eat fruits, vegetables, nuts, beans, olive oil, intact grains, and garlic every day," Junelle says. "If these form the foundation of their diet, they don't have to worry about following a strict food plan."

THE ANTI-INFLAMMATORY DIET MAKES
the FOLLOWING RECOMMENDATIONS

EAT FREQUENTLY

VEGETABLES: Both raw and cooked, from across the color spectrum, organic if possible; 4–5 servings daily

FRUITS: Fresh in season or frozen, organic if possible; 3–4 servings daily

WHOLE GRAINS: Intact, not pulverized, such as brown rice, barley, quinoa, and steel-cut oatmeal; 3–5 servings daily

BEANS AND LEGUMES: 1–2 servings daily

HEALTHY FATS: Extra-virgin olive oil, nuts (especially walnuts), avocado, and seeds like flaxseed; 5–7 servings a day

WHOLE SOY FOODS: Edamame, miso, soy milk, tofu, tempeh; 1–2 servings a day

TEA: White, green, oolong; 2–4 cups a day

RED WINE (optional): 1–2 glasses a day

UNLIMITED AMOUNTS OF ASIAN MUSHROOMS AND HEALTHY HERBS AND SPICES (garlic, turmeric, ginger, cinnamon)

DAILY SUPPLEMENTS

EAT REGULARLY
(on a weekly basis)

WHOLE WHEAT PASTA: (al dente) 2–3 times a week

FISH AND SEAFOOD: Wild Alaskan salmon, Alaskan black cod, sardines; 2–6 times a week

OTHER SOURCES OF PROTEIN: High-quality natural cheeses and yogurt, omega-3–enriched eggs, skinless poultry, lean meats; 1–2 times a week

EAT SPARINGLY

HEALTHY SWEETS such as plain dark chocolate

The idea behind this food plan is that instead of eliminating certain foods—which often has the effect of making us crave what we know we can't have—we should instead build our meals around the more desirable foods on the list above. It's a gradual shift of intention, but a powerful one, since in the course of emphasizing some foods, others naturally become less dominant in our diets. If we're eating more whole grains, we're almost automatically eating fewer refined, processed carbohydrates. If we introduce more nuts and beans into our diet, we're shifting our diet toward plant proteins and away from animal ones. Likewise with fats—as we increase the number of plant-based fats in our diet like olive oil, nuts, flaxseeds, and avocados, we're by default reducing the amount of butter and cheese.

The important thing is that the anti-inflammatory food plan is not meant to be restrictive. "It's fine to have a piece of birthday cake now and then," says Junelle, "or to have an omelet if you go out to brunch. We're talking about the way you eat most of the time."

Chakra Meditation

is functioning optimally to create a rounded sense of health—much like all of the colors of the spectrum glowing in harmony.

The purpose of a chakra meditation is to check in systematically with these seven bodily centers so that you can evaluate where you feel calm and relaxed and which chakras are holding tension. You begin by sitting or lying in a comfortable position and allowing your breath to become gentle and rhythmic. You can either work from the top down—from the crown chakra at the top of your head to the root chakra at the base of your spine—or vice versa. Some practitioners like to end on the more diffuse energy of the crown chakra, others with the more grounded energy of the root chakra. It makes sense to try both and see which works better for you. But for the purposes of our example, we will move from bottom to top. As you direct your attention to each chakra in turn, visualize energy emanating from that chakra in the designated color.

The **ROOT CHAKRA** is located at the base of the spine and associated with the color red. When it is blocked, we feel disconnected from the physical world, impractical, and "unrooted." When it's open, we feel physically energetic, present, and engaged in our environment.

The **NAVEL CHAKRA** is located in the lower abdomen and associated with the color orange. This is the pleasure chakra, the home of passion, and when it is blocked, we may feel uncomfortable expressing our

The chakras are seven energy focal points located along the center meridian of the body, with each chakra corresponding to a different color on the spectrum and a certain kind of physical and spiritual energy. When a chakra becomes blocked, that energy can no longer circulate, creating health imbalances, which can take the form of headaches, body pain, muscle tension, and overall fatigue. When all of the chakras are open, in contrast, each part of the body sexual selves. When it is open, we are vital lovers in every sense of the word—not just romantically, but in terms of our capacity to enjoy the many sensual pleasures of life.

The **SOLAR PLEXUS** is located just above the navel in the center of the torso and is associated with the color yellow. Concentration, control, power, and authority emanate from this chakra. When it is blocked, we may lack confidence and self-control. When it is open, we are the masters of our own lives, able to direct our energies at will.

The **HEART CHAKRA** is found in the middle of our chest and is associated with the color green. The heart chakra emanates compassion, forgiveness, and understanding. When it is closed, our relationships suffer. When it is open, we feel a deep sense of connection with our families, friends, and partners and with all of the beings of the world.

The **THROAT CHAKRA**, not surprisingly, is located in the throat and is associated with the color sky blue. It is the chakra of communication and determines the way in which we speak our personal truth. If it is blocked, we may have trouble telling others how we really feel, but when it is open, our personal knowledge, wisdom, and kindness pour through.

The **BROW CHAKRA** is the imaginary "third eye" in the middle of the forehead, and it is associated with the color indigo. It governs intuition and imagination, and when it is blocked, we may feel creatively blocked as well. But when it is open, we gain full access to our intuitive insights and our creativity blossoms.

Finally, the **CROWN CHAKRA** is located at the top of the head and is associated with the color violet, although some chakra meditations prefer describing it as a clear light, which is a combination of all of the colors of the spectrum blended together. This is the chakra of spirituality, and when it is open, we are mindful, conscious, and at one with the universe. When it is closed, we feel earthbound and uninspired, cut off from our sources of higher wisdom.

It's easy to see how a chakra meditation serves as a type of self-therapy, showing us precisely what's lacking in our lives. Perhaps your throat chakra feels open and comfortable, indicating you have no trouble communicating with words, but if your navel chakra seems equally blocked, you may have trouble demonstrating physical affection. People who feel open in the higher chakras but blocked in the lower may be too spacey to make their dreams reality; those who feel comfortable with the lower chakras and less so with the upper might need to retreat from the physical world and explore the more spiritual side of their lives.

Q10 (COQ10): 90–120 milligrams daily, for the heart

VITAMIN D: 1,000 units D3 (Sunscreen has done great things for our skin-cancer rates but has left many Americans significantly deficient in vitamin D.)

OMEGA-3 FATTY ACIDS: 1,000 milligrams each day, combined from DHA and EPA

EATING for WEIGHT LOSS

Determining your caloric needs is a simple equation on paper. You start by adding up the number of calories you burn in a typical day, which is a combination of your resting metabolic rate and the number of calories you burn through activity. Then you tally the number of calories you consume daily through food. If you burn less than you consume, you gain weight. If you burn more than you consume, you lose weight.

But, as discussed in the January chapter on exercise, the fact that we all know this intellectually doesn't necessarily make it any easier to actually attain. For starters, most of us guess wrong on our numbers. *Way wrong.* We tend to overestimate how many calories we're burning and underestimate how many calories we're eating, and thus we're bewildered as to why our weight keeps sneaking higher and higher.

Guests at Miraval have the opportunity to get a much more accurate read on their personal numbers. They can have their resting metabolic rate tested by Junelle—a simple evaluation of an overnight fast followed by a measurement based on the client's rate of respiration. That number is then adjusted to reflect how many calories they burn in routine activity; a kindergarten teacher probably burns more calories a day than a deskbound accountant. "You have to ask some questions to get a good read on this," says Junelle. "Do they live in the city? Do they walk to work? Do they have a dog who needs exercise? Do they go up and down stairs all day?" And finally, they can have their aerobic capacity tested by Andrew Wolf in his Optimal Fitness Diagnostic to see what sort of caloric burn they're getting from their daily workouts.

The combination of these three figures gives the guest a pretty solid estimate of how many calories they're burning in a typical day. "When the evaluations are done, I sit down with them to discuss the results," says Junelle. "They may have been thinking they're burning 2,500 calories a day, and they're wondering why they're not losing weight. I often have to say something like, 'No, your actual energy output is more like 1,700 a day.'"

So what does it mean to eat less than 1,700 calories a day? "A number is just data," says Junelle. "I have them talk me through a day in their life and tell what they're eating automatically now. Most people eat out at least one meal per day, and you can get your whole 1,700 calories at lunch in just one of those overstuffed sandwiches at a fast-food place. I show them what a serving of bread is supposed

EXERCISE
Water Conditioning

Few exercises are as versatile as water conditioning. Because the cushioning resistance of the water makes it so easy on the joints, pool exercise has long been touted as the perfect activity for older people, pregnant women, and athletes recovering from an injury. But this isn't just your mother's workout. Water conditioning can be fiercely aerobic; if you add kickboxing and dance-inspired moves to your routine, you can get your heart pumping.

At Miraval, instructors look for ways to keep the class fun. You might salsa and samba along with Latin music, straddle noodles like horses for a lap around the pool, or square off against other exercisers in relay races, where the lighthearted competition distracts you from how hard you're really working. The pool is also the perfect environment for stretching and joint mobility work and surprisingly good for strength training as well. If you add foam rubber dumbbells or resistance gloves to your workout, you can build muscle along with cardio endurance.

So an exercise that hits cardio, strength, and flexibility all in one—and is fun besides? It's no wonder that water conditioning is one of the most popular exercise classes at Miraval.

AT HOME: Try a fun water class at a gym near you or create your own in your pool at home with your personal choice of music.

to look like, and they realize that those huge buns are two servings of starch, maybe three. I show them what four ounces of protein looks like, and they realize they were getting eight ounces on that sandwich. It can be a sobering moment when they realize they're spending their whole caloric allotment for the day on one routine meal."

This is where the anti-inflammatory diet comes into play, since you get more bang for your caloric buck by building your diet around fruits and vegetables, which tend to be naturally low in calories. Even the anti-inflammatory foods that are higher in calories such as nuts, beans, avocados, and whole grains are likely to keep you satisfied much longer than their processed and refined counterparts. Whole foods tend to be higher in fiber and take longer to metabolize; a bowl of vegetable chili and a salad will likely not only have fewer calories than that overstuffed sandwich, but the odds are you won't feel the need to snack three hours later.

But no matter how smart you are about making better food choices, it can still be challenging to meet your nutritional needs on 1,700 calories a day. "If 1,700 looks too restrictive and they're discouraged," says Junelle, "that's when I suggest they talk to an exercise physiologist, like Andrew Wolf. This is the point where people realize that they want to be able to eat more like 2,000 calories a day and still lose weight. And in order to do that, they have to increase their level of exercise as well as change their diet. One really never works for long without the other."

MAXIMIZE YOUR BIOLOGICAL AGE

We've all met people who are 55 but who look and act a decade younger, maybe even two. Likewise, we all know people whose biological age is higher than their chronological age, whose lifestyle choices have made them seem older than they actually are. "I rarely use the term 'anti-aging,'" says Junelle. "I prefer to say 'maximize your biological age' because the goal should be healthy aging. So I encourage people to commit to feeling as good as they can for as long as they can,

and a lot of that depends on what they eat."

Genetics do play a role in how well we age, but not as big a role as once thought. "You're not doomed to high cholesterol or diabetes by your family history alone," says Junelle. "Our lifestyle choices are largely within our control, and if you don't take the time to eat well and exercise, that's your choice."

Junelle lists five things you can do to maximize your biological age:

1. Follow an anti-inflammatory diet with an emphasis on whole foods.

2. Exercise regularly, implementing cardio, weight-bearing, and stretching routines into your program.

3. Concentrate on getting restful sleep.

4. Find a stress-reduction method that works for you, and practice it daily.

5. Incorporate supplements based on your personal nutritional needs.

BUT WHAT DO WE DO about the KIDS?

As any parent knows, food can become a family battleground, whether it's the six-month-old who spits out carrots or the 16-year-old who has developed the worrisome tendency to skip breakfast.

"When it comes to kids, the best thing you can do is expose them to good food choices," says Junelle. "You can't make them put certain things in their body and

leave others out, but you can create a good environment that makes healthy eating easier."

For example, Junelle points out that it's one thing to buy a bag of grapes and just leave them in a bag in the back of the fridge hoping the kids will find them. "Take them home, wash them, and leave them in a bowl on the counter," she says. "Make it easy for everyone to grab

a few as they're passing through the kitchen. You can also encourage the kids to help you cook, even when they're very young. Kids love to make pizza, and when you do it yourself with whole-wheat dough and veggies it can be far more nutritious than what you'd buy in the store."

HOW to IMPLEMENT the PLAN

If you're feeling overwhelmed at this point, that's normal. "My clients often leave my office with many recommendations," says Junelle, "but I suggest that when they get home they start by implementing just one at a time. Maybe it's making a conscious effort to increase their fruit and vegetable intake, to get more color in their salads. Then move on to address the supplement issue. Next they might want to limit their use of land-based protein."

"The idea is to make changes in a way that's not so huge, and you certainly don't want to feel like you're being punished. If a family is used to eating pasta two or three nights a week, one night they might want to make it a whole grain. It's a slight adjustment to remember to put on the brown rice right when you get home from work because it takes 40 minutes to cook instead of six minutes in the microwave. Replace beans for your protein one night a week. Find a recipe for a new kind of guacamole. Go to a farmers' market one weekend, and plan your meals around the produce you find there. Or if you're headed to the grocery, tell yourself that for this one shopping trip you'll choose everything that goes into your basket based on what's in it instead of what isn't in it. Small changes count."

KEY POINTS FOR MAY

✿ Forget old-fashioned diets with a long list of forbidden foods. For both health and weight loss, it's more important to focus on what you're putting into your body than on what you're leaving out.

✿ The anti-inflammatory food plan is the new dietary standard. It encourages you to eat more fruits, vegetables, whole grains, and legumes, while reducing your intake of animal protein and processed foods.

✿ Color-spectrum eating is a nutritional "cheat sheet." By choosing fruits and vegetables from across the color spectrum, you ensure that you're meeting your nutritional needs.

JUNELLE LUPIANI, R.D.

Junelle is a registered dietitian who specializes in weight management and the integration of nutrition for disease treatment and prevention. She believes that eating well is far easier than most people imagine and can have a very powerful effect on keeping you healthy for the rest of your life. Her mission is to provide practical advice to achieve optimal health.

QUINOA SALAD in RADICCHIO CUPS

If you think a salad can't be hearty, think again. Quinoa is a nutritional bonanza—high in both protein and fiber, while also being gluten-free and easy to digest. It's a favorite with Miraval guests who, once they learn how to pronounce it (keen-wah), fall in love with its versatility and rich nutty flavor. Quinoa is often described as a grain, but it's actually a seed and more closely related to beets and spinach than to cereals.

In the recipe below, the quinoa is served chilled, and the addition of red and yellow tomatoes and the green of the parsley and mint expand the color spectrum and raise the nutritional benefits even higher. Spooning the mixture into pretty little radicchio cups gives you maximum presentation with minimal fuss, and this salad transports well, making it a great contribution to a picnic or group supper.

MAKES 2 CUPS; SERVING SIZE: ½ CUP

1 c. quinoa, uncooked
½ c. cucumber, peeled, seeded, and chopped
½ c. vine-ripened red and yellow tomatoes, chopped
2 Tbsp. fresh mint, chopped
1 Tbsp. extra-virgin olive oil
4 Tbsp. fresh-squeezed lemon juice (2 average-sized lemons)
2 Tbsp. Italian parsley, chopped
¼ Tbsp. salt
1 Tbsp. pepper
Radicchio lettuce cups, eight leaves

Preheat saucepan over high heat for 45 seconds. Add dry quinoa to pan (no oil). Stir to toast, about 1 minute. The quinoa will begin to crackle and smell a little like popcorn.

Add 2 cups water and bring to a boil. Reduce the heat to low, cover, and simmer until tender, 10 to 12 minutes. (The quinoa will expand during the cooking process.) Remove the pan from the heat, drain any excess liquid, allow to cool gradually, and then chill in the refrigerator.

When the quinoa has been chilled, toss it with all other ingredients except the radicchio; adjust seasonings to taste. For best flavor, allow to sit for 15 minutes before serving. Arrange radicchio cups on each plate and spoon ½ cup of salad into the cups.

CALORIES: 150; TOTAL FAT: 5 G; CARBOHYDRATES: 20 G; DIETARY FIBER: 3 G; PROTEIN: 4 G

NAT

June

NATURE One of the most enchanting things about Miraval is its location. The Sonoran Desert is teeming with life; javelina, jackrabbits, roadrunners, and hummingbirds dot the Miraval property. The guest rooms are named in honor of the intriguing variety of cacti: yucca, ocotillo, mesquite, saguaro. But the plants, animals, canyons, and mountains are more than just a stunning backdrop to the activities of Miraval. The wonders of nature have much to teach us about human nature.

SPA

Abhyanga

Abhyanga is an ancient healing therapy designed to restore a sense of balance in the body. The treatment is a delight for the senses as warm, herb-infused oils are massaged into the skin with a light touch. Oils are especially helpful in promoting the lymphatic system and encouraging the release of toxins, so Abhyanga is an excellent therapy for reducing muscle soreness and tension, as well as calming the central nervous system.

Once the toxins are released, the skin can then begin to more efficiently absorb nutrients and carry them to the cells. So it's a matter of toxins out and nutrients in, with the oil serving to lubricate and protect the skin during the process. In the more extensive treatment Ultimate Ayurvedic, guests are wrapped in a warm cocoon of towels while a slow stream of gently heated oil is directed to the "third eye" in the middle of their forehead. The "mama points" of the body are addressed, since they are key meridians that, when opened through the application of essential oils, promote profound feelings of release and calm.

There's a reason why Abhyanga, in its various forms, is one of the most popular treatments at Miraval. The massage is incredibly soothing, and the warm oil penetrates deeply into both your skin and hair, leaving you soft and smooth after the treatment. Miraval regulars often schedule Abhyanga at night; not only does it transition you into a wonderful evening of sleep but you can also leave the oil in your hair and on your skin overnight for maximum absorption.

AYURVEDA ABHYANGA

The practice of Ayurveda stresses a balance of three elemental energies called doshas: vāta, pitta, and kapha.

VĀTA is associated with bodily functions with motion, including blood circulation and breathing.

PITTA is associated with the body's metabolic systems, including digestion and temperature.

KAPHA supplies water to all body parts and the skin and maintains the immune system.

The goal of Ayurveda is to attain and maintain balance in all three doshas through the use of plant-based treatments, exercise, yoga, meditation, and maintaining a healthy lifestyle.

Abhyanga Massage is performed by rubbing the skin with herbal oil to increase blood circulation and draw toxins out of the body through the skin.

HOME CARE: It is easy to perform an Abhyanga massage at home. You can incorporate this practice into your daily shower as you cleanse and as you apply your moisturizer. To increase circulation in the skin and muscles, apply the product in an upward stroke toward the heart/lymph nodes (that is, elbow to shoulder, wrist to elbow, etc.). To do a true Ayurveda balancing treatment, you will want to use sesame oil (vāta), coconut oil (pitta), and olive oil (kapha). You can also warm the oil!

IN OTHER WORDS . . . IT'S NOT about the HORSE

It's these very first moments of working with the horse that often provide the information needed for transformation. They give the person the chance to observe how he or she reacts in a dynamic where the other party—in this case, the horse—isn't responding favorably to their expectations.

"Horses are the perfect creatures for this kind of work because they don't want anything from humans," Wyatt says. "They're not like dogs running up wagging their tails, trying to please us. A horse looks at a human and he feels one of two things, either safety or fear. If we give him a clear directive, he's safe. If we're unclear, he won't feel safe. So if when we take his leg in our hand, our intention isn't clear, he won't lift his hoof and that's that. You can't do anything to convince him. He won't move until you're sending out a clear intention."

Over three decades ago, when Wyatt was wrestling with his own demons, a therapist told him that his ability to overcome addiction and find joy in his life depended upon one solitary thing: Was he willing to do something different? The people in the Equine Experience aren't necessarily facing drug addiction or alcoholism, but everyone comes to the dusty arena with their own struggles. How they react when the horse won't lift his hoof is a microcosm for how they react to many troubles in life, and the challenge, just as it was for Wyatt years ago, is learning how to do something differently.

"We've all been conditioned to seek external validation," says Wyatt. "We believe that the way people treat us tells us who we are—which is why we can become agitated when the horse won't do what we want him to do. We go through life wondering what others think of us, whether or not they like us or respect us, and we tell ourselves stories about why they act toward us in the way they do."

Our focus on external validation has two very bad side effects. As mentioned before, being obsessed with how others view us can cause us to behave manipulatively. "When we're trying to 'get' someone to like us, love us, or respect us, we've forfeited the chance to really connect with them in a meaningful way," says Wyatt. "If we hide our true feelings and invent a different version of ourselves, one who we think others will approve of, we are in fact committing spiritual suicide. Our original self is the best we have to offer to our world. This has to be accepted for healing to take place."

All this external focus also keeps us from accessing our inner wisdom and learning anything about ourselves. "When we're looking to other people to tell us we are okay," says Wyatt, "we're disconnected from our own emotions. As a culture, we're trained to ignore the most important relationship we'll ever have, the one we have with ourselves. People can go through all kinds of therapy and be very educated but still never have learned how to pay attention to what they really think and feel. They don't see all the ways those thoughts and feelings are dictating the way they live and probably screwing up their lives."

"When we're trying to 'get' someone to like us, love us, or respect us, we've forfeited the chance to really connect with them in a meaningful way."

Hiking

The grounds of Miraval are so lush and beautiful that everyone enjoys walking them, and if you're up for more exercise and adventure, there are also a variety of guided hikes that leave every morning.

The A and B level hikes take place in the hills behind Miraval property. "Our location is so great that you just walk out back and within minutes you're in nature," says Neil McLeod, head of the Outdoor Adventure Program at Miraval. The A level hikes cover three to five miles and last an average of two hours. The B level hikes cover the same gently rolling terrain but are longer, usually lasting about three hours. In both cases, tennis shoes are fine, and Miraval provides waist packs and water bottles for hikers.

If you're seeking more challenge, there are C level hikes in which guests leave the property and travel in the Miraval bus to parks and trails around the Tucson area. You may be gone as long as five hours overall, with at least three of those spent walking, and there will be significant gains in elevation. D level hikes add rock- and mountain-climbing elements with sharp vertical ascents and are designed for experienced climbers. For C and D level trips, hiking boots are recommended.

No matter what level of hiking you choose, you can expect beautiful views, a great workout, and the camaraderie of your group and leaders. But remember that the altitude of Tucson (starting at about 2,500 feet and gaining elevation from there) can make the hikes a little more strenuous than expected for guests who live at lower elevations. It's a good idea to train a bit at home before you go and give yourself a day to acclimate to the environment before you hike.

IN OTHER WORDS . . . IT'S NOT
about OTHER PEOPLE

Many of the people who sign up for the Equine Experience show up with a friend, spouse, or sibling; and along with the self-realizations, the exercises often reveal the dynamics of their relationship. "If you and the other person are playing some kind of game, working with the horse will bust that game," Wyatt says. "I've had wives come up to me furious and saying, 'He treats that horse just like he treats me.' And maybe the husband sees that he only has one coping skill that he's using for all situations, and he'll say, 'Oh God, I didn't know I was doing that.' We all keep doing the same stuff in life over and over again with no awareness of where it's coming from or how it seems to affect other people. But there's no place to hide with the horse. You can tell a lot from who's more at ease with the horse, who he'll trot along for and who makes him dig in his heels. Whether it's two sisters, or a husband and wife, or friends, whatever hasn't been dealt with in their relationship presents itself, usually in the first five minutes."

Working with the horse can also help each person in the relationship to recognize and claim their own role in whatever dynamic exists between them. If there's disagreement or conflict, we've been taught to direct the blame at others. *If only he would understand . . . If only she didn't always react like this . . . How can I be happy when you're driving me crazy?*

"That's our favorite," Wyatt says with an impish grin. "Claiming that other people are driving us crazy. The truth is, you were crazy before you met them. What's crazy is going around believing that what other people say and do should have the power to control the quality of our day. But there's a payoff in being focused on other people and expecting them to tell us who we are: We can go a long time without really having to face ourselves. But in the Equine Experience, even though the people may be paired up to work with a horse, each one of them is having his or her own experience, and whether they believe it or not, each person is 100 percent responsible for 50 percent of every relationship she or he chooses to be in."

Wyatt also offers Equine Intensives several times a year, which are four-day retreats where guests spend most of their Miraval stay at the ranch working with the horses and interacting with the other guests in the program. "The work goes much deeper than the three-hour Equine Experience," Wyatt says, "and while it takes some courage, people can begin to take responsibility for their lives and to change the patterns that aren't working. In each group, there's always someone who mirrors for you exactly what you need to work on. Your conflict with them is a gift, because you can help each other heal. We offer the tools, support, and safety so that people can start to reclaim who they are and reclaim the joy that they've lost along the way. But just like the name says, it's intense, and every participant is in charge of how deep the work goes. I won't push you, but I will hold your hand and jump with you."

Once again, the horse is the perfect medium for the message. "Many of our guests have their defenses up so high they won't surrender them to any therapist," Wyatt says. "But most people feel safe with animals. They just don't have as complicated a history with animals, so if their life has been so rough that their trust levels are shot to hell with people, this is a good way to start. If they learn to connect with the horse, ultimately they can take those same routes to learn to reconnect with people."

But even if someone doesn't come to the Intensive with a history of trauma, working with a horse can still be a safe zone to explore patterns that are causing pain and isolation in their lives. "People have learned a lot during those four days," Wyatt says. "They may see that they're not as damaged and flawed as they thought they were. A lot of their fear and self-doubt may have come from somewhere else, from things people told them a long time ago that turned into the stories they've carried around in their head. They've been waiting for others to tell them what matters in their life, what's okay. Releasing that can be painful, but on the other side is empowerment and joy. People who have completed the Intensive often return to Miraval or write us, and they often say that they went home and made significant decisions, producing major changes in their lives."

But people who don't have access to horses, the desert, and the Equine Experience . . . what can they do?

"Remember, the horse is just a metaphor," Wyatt says. "You don't really need him because you are witness to your thoughts, feelings, and behavior every day. Most of us keep running into the same obstacles over and over. I tell people, 'Just pay attention to what you think, what you feel, and how you behave. Look at what keeps coming up for you. You don't have to have a 1,200-pound horse showing you the results of your behavior. Look at how you drive a car, how you cook dinner, how you talk to your child, how you create or cope with conflict.' We all have recurring patterns of behavior that are practically screaming at us that this is how we cope with life circumstances. Through the process of questioning or confronting these behaviors, we cease to be at the mercy of the external 'how it's supposed to be' and begin to arrive at 'how it is.' Only then is it possible to reclaim who we truly are and change our lives."

KEY POINTS FOR JUNE

✿ The way you do one thing is the way you do everything. Mindfully noting how you drive a car or interact with your kids can give you insight into your whole approach to life.

✿ We are often beset by fear and self-doubt because our culture has taught us to seek external validation in the form of money, fame, success, and the approval of other people. But we only attain true joy by learning to access our inner wisdom.

✿ Being authentic requires us to give up our ideas of "how it's supposed to be" and acknowledge "how it is." Only then can we really embrace change and improve our lives.

WYATT WEBB, Creator,
The Miraval Equine Experience™

What began as a facilitated experimental group with emphasis on in-depth relationship skills examination has evolved into Miraval's Equine Experience. In a safe and supportive setting, people correct false belief systems about themselves and remember who they truly are. Wyatt is the author of It's Not about the Horse; *What to Do When You Don't Know What to Do: Common Horse Sense; and* Five Steps for Overcoming Fear and Self-Doubt: Journey into Present-Moment Time. *Wyatt began his career touring North America as a professional performer for 15 years. For more than 25 years he has worked with adults, adolescents, families, couples, and corporations in a therapeutic setting. Wyatt has a B.A. from West Georgia College.*

PISTACHIO-MUSHROOM DUXELLES STUFFED ROASTED POBLANO CHILI with RED PEPPER COULIS

We'll admit something right up front: This is definitely the most labor-intensive of the recipes featured in this book. You peel, roast, and then stuff the poblano chili with a pistachio and mushroom mixture, and then the entire dish is drizzled with a red pepper coulis. This poblano chili ends up being so flavorful and colorful that it will convince you, once and for all, that there really is such a thing as healthy Mexican cuisine that tastes terrific. So invite over some friends, open a bottle of wine, divvy up the tasks, and take your sweet time going through every step of the dish. Trust us, you won't be sorry.

MAKES 4 SERVINGS

4 whole-roasted poblano chili peppers, seeds removed

1 c. Pistachio-Mushroom Duxelles *(recipe follows)*

1 c. Red Pepper Coulis *(recipe follows)*

1 Tbsp. Cotija cheese

ROAST THE CHILIS Turn gas burner on high. Using a pair of tongs, carefully place the pepper on the burner. Leave pepper on the flame until skin is charred completely black and no original color is left. Rotate to the next side and repeat until the entire pepper is charred black, about 24 minutes.

Use the tongs to remove the pepper from the flame and place in a Ziplock or paper bag. Seal the bag to make sure that no steam can escape, and let the pepper rest for 8–10 minutes. This will allow the hot steam inside of the pepper to slowly loosen the charred skin as it cools. Please note that the pepper, and therefore the bag, will be extremely hot after being removed from the flame. Even after the pepper is cool to the touch, there may still be steam inside of the pepper hot enough to burn you. Once the pepper is cool enough to touch, lightly massage it through the bag to remove most of the skin.

Split roasted chilis along one side to remove the seeds, but make sure to keep chili intact, including stem, so that it can be stuffed with the duxelles and cheese.

Stuff with duxelles-Cotija filling.

Preheat oven to 350°F, place stuffed peppers on lightly oiled baking sheet, and bake for 15 minutes, or until heated all of the way through.

To plate, ladle a quarter cup of red pepper coulis into the center of each of the four plates, and use a spatula to transfer the stuffed chili peppers to each plate, on top of the sauce.

CALORIES: 184; TOTAL FAT: 12 G; CARBOHYDRATES: 15 G; DIETARY FIBER: 2 G; PROTEIN: 8 G

PISTACHIO-MUSHROOM DUXELLES

MAKES 2 CUPS

SERVING SIZE: ½ CUP

½ lb. (2 large) portobello mushrooms, gills removed, with stems

½ lb. (18 medium) shiitake mushrooms, stems removed

3 Tbsp. dry-roasted pistachio nuts

½ c. red bell pepper, roughly chopped

2 tsp. shallots, chopped

1 tsp. garlic, chopped

2 Tbsp. madeira or dry sherry

1 tsp. Miraval Oil Blend (3:1 mix of canola oil and extra-virgin olive oil)

¼ tsp. kosher salt

⅛ tsp. freshly ground black pepper

To toast pistachios, spread out on baking sheet and roast at 350°F for about 5 minutes, or until the pistachios become fragrant.

Add all ingredients except madeira to food processor and process to a medium dice.

In a medium saucepan, sauté mixture over medium heat for about 1 minute 30 seconds. Deglaze with madeira, reduce heat, and simmer over low heat while stirring constantly, until mixture softens and liquid is evaporated, about 4 minutes.

Remove from saucepan, and spread out on plate or small casserole dish to chill, and reserve for service. This mixture may be refrigerated for up to 2 days.

RED PEPPER COULIS

MAKES 1 CUP

SERVING SIZE: ¼ CUP

2 large red bell peppers, roasted, peeled, and chopped

½ c. yellow onion, chopped

½ tsp. Miraval Oil Blend (3:1 mix of canola oil and extra-virgin olive oil)

1 Tbsp. fresh garlic, minced

2 tsp. fresh oregano, chopped

1½ Tbsp. cilantro, chopped

1½ c. vegetable stock or water

1½ tsp. cornstarch mixed with 1½ tsp. water

¼ tsp. kosher salt

¼ tsp. freshly ground black pepper

Heat a saucepan over medium heat, and add the oil to coat the bottom of the pan. Stir in the roasted peppers, onion, garlic, oregano, and cilantro; cook until the onion has softened, approximately 2 minutes. Add the stock or water and simmer for 12 to 15 minutes.

Carefully ladle the pepper mixture into a blender and process until smooth. Strain the pepper mixture through a colander lined with cheesecloth or a fine-mesh strainer.

Pour the strained mixture back into the saucepan, and bring to a low boil. Mix in the cornstarch and cook, stirring constantly, until the sauce thickens and coats the back of the spoon. Season with salt and black pepper.

Use the sauce immediately, or cool down in an ice bath. Store in an airtight container for up to 1 week in the refrigerator or about 1 month in the freezer.

July

CHALLENGE Do you think of *challenge* as a scary word? The dictionary defines it as "calling for the full use of one's abilities in a difficult but stimulating effort." Unfortunately, we often get so bogged down in the "difficult" part of the definition that we overlook the "stimulating" part and forget that challenges can be absorbing, intriguing, exciting, and most of all, fun.

Challenge can take many forms, from the physical challenge of a tough workout to the emotional challenge of confronting an issue in a marriage to the mental challenge of approaching an old problem in a new way. But what they all have in common is that they reward us richly for the risks we take. Even if the situation doesn't turn out as expected, and even if there are a few butterflies along the way, rising to a challenge always builds our confidence and shows us that we're able to do much more than we thought.

Forgiveness

When we first think about it, forgiveness meditation might seem like a kitten—soft and gentle and fuzzy.

But in reality, it's more of a tiger.

In fact, forgiving ourselves and others can be one of the most challenging of all spiritual practices, bringing us face-to-face with a variety of dark emotions, including bitterness, regret, guilt, or rage. But forgiveness is also an essential foundation of meditation practice, since it's difficult, if not impossible, to expand our mindfulness and ability to live in the present moment when we're haunted by events from the past.

The forgiveness meditation at Miraval has three parts: asking forgiveness from those you may have hurt, granting forgiveness to those who have hurt you, and finally, asking and granting forgiveness

for the ways in which you've hurt yourself. We can't expect to develop compassion for others until we've developed compassion for ourselves.

To start, sit or lie comfortably, close your eyes, and let your breath become natural. After you have become relaxed, begin to recite, either silently or out loud, these words: "If I have hurt or harmed anyone, knowingly or unknowingly, I ask for their forgiveness." As images, people, or memories arise, release the burden of your guilt and ask them for forgiveness.

The second step is offering forgiveness to those who have harmed you. Memories or images of people may again arise, and there's a good chance that you won't feel the actual emotion of forgiveness immediately. That's fine. Forgiveness meditation is not about glossing over our psychological wounds with pretty words, and it's certainly not about faking an emotion you don't feel. It is about our intention to forgive and our desire to let go of any anger or bitterness that we still hold so that these emotions will no longer limit our lives. As the faces of people or memories arise in your mind, you can say, silently, *I forgive you,* or if that doesn't seem appropriate, simply hold the image and observe the emotion around it.

Finally, turn your attention to forgiving yourself. Now memories may arise about mistakes you have made or ways that you've harmed yourself through addictions, compulsions, repetitive behavior, or bad decisions. We all have times in which we've failed to love ourselves and have instead judged ourselves harshly, using the sort of critical language we would never direct at a friend. Forgiveness meditation can be the first step in letting go of any tendency toward self-wounding and all of the ways we've showed unkindness to ourselves throughout our lives.

Don't expect forgiveness on any of the three levels to be immediate. For most people, forgiveness meditation evolves in its own way and at its own pace. The important thing is to put your intention to forgive out into the world on a consistent basis and to observe how your feelings around the issue change over time.

course before they do the challenge and 'check it out,' and there are always a few more who have lots of questions. They can see the cables and the ropes, and we explain everything about it to them so they understand it's completely safe. But it can still be hard to relax into that understanding during the moments when you're actually confronting the fear. Talking about statistical probability isn't going to comfort you then. I've seen people at the zip line, for instance, who manage to step off the platform, which is the scary part, but who never really relax into the harness for the ride. They spend the whole trip gripping the strap as if that can somehow magically keep them in control."

The group dynamic is a little different at each challenge. Neil says people are often guarded at introductions, and the seemingly simple question of "Who's going to go first?" is actually the point where the challenge begins. "Some people like to plunge in and go first," Neil says. "It can make them look like the bravest in the crew, but it's actually their way of making sure they don't have to wait until their anxiety gradually grows to unmanageable proportions. If people volunteer to go first, we suggest they experiment with going last, because shaking up their normal patterns of behavior is exactly what will take them out of their comfort zone. Other people naturally like to hang back and watch everyone else go before them. They're the perfectionists, trying to gauge what the others do, analyze it, and perfect their own technique. Guess what? They go first."

Scrambling the sequence isn't a mean trick on the part of the challenge team; it's a way to get everyone out of their default mode and make sure they treat the challenge as an experiment in doing things differently. "Most people aren't adrenaline junkies," says Neil, "so a carefully monitored challenge at a resort like Miraval is a way for them to dip a toe into the whole arena of extreme activities. They may think the challenge is just the part where they swing out on the rope or walk across the beam, but each step in the activity from the introductions to the sequencing is designed to make them slightly uncomfortable without ever being unsafe."

The partnership formed by being nervous together and then working together is also an important part of the experience. "During the long minutes of waiting their turn, watching others, or in some cases helping them through the challenge, and finally going through the experience themselves, people open up to a surprising degree," says Neil. "When you bring a group of strangers together in a stressful situation, that stress will break down any barriers between them, and they'll support each other easily. The group often forms a surprising degree of unity, with people who may have otherwise never met walking away as friends.

"Guests bring their individual goals to the challenges, but my goal each time is to form a community," Neil says. "One of the reasons people are often reserved at the beginning of the challenge is that they think they're the only one who is scared. They think they're the only one who couldn't sleep the night before, or that their story is the most dramatic or painful one out there. In the course of the challenge, they see other people's fears and hear their stories, and in circumstances like this, even a few hours together are enough to create a bond. The challenges can help people develop compassion —both for other people, which is usually the easy part, and also for themselves."

One of the most important parts of the challenge activity begins just when it seems that it's all over. When the task is complete and the participants are all back on the ground and unstrapped from their safety gear, the team leads them in a debriefing where they talk about their experiences. Where else in their lives have they felt similar emotions—such as being stuck, reluctant to rely on someone else, uncertain of what the next step should be, or afraid to let go? "Challenge without reflection is just an adrenaline rush," says Neil.

"It's fun, but it fades." That's why it's important to pause for a moment just after the experience, before your conscious, cautious mind has kicked back in, and think about what the challenge has shown you about yourself and how you might apply these realizations to your daily life back home.

But what surprises many people the most isn't the way they felt when they were scared or stuck—after all, they're used to those

feelings—but the sense of sheer exhilaration that comes with having pushed through and completed the challenge. "If they open themselves up to the experience," Neil says, "they'll probably walk away saying, 'That felt good, I want more of that.' And that's why we're really doing this, to help people become more comfortable in taking chances and tolerating the unknown in all areas of their lives."

TYPES of CHALLENGES

QUANTUM LEAP In Quantum Leap, Miraval's original and most famous challenge, you climb up a 25-foot telephone pole, step up to a plate-sized disk on top, pause, and then leap. Belay ropes catch you after a partial drop and then slowly lower you down back to the ground. "For most people climbing onto the disk and standing up is the most challenging part," says Neil. "They often report that the actual jump is very freeing." There's also a Quantum Leap II where the platform, on which two guests at a time can stand, is 35 feet in the air.

A SWING AND A PRAYER This is one of the more physically passive challenges, since guests are strapped into a harness and pulled up into the air by a rope pulley system controlled by their fellow team members. The guest enjoys the view for as long as he likes and then, when he's ready, releases a rope for a massive swing into midair. "In some ways, this may seem like more of a ride than a challenge," says Neil. "But for people who have to be in control all the time, trusting others to lift them and then letting go of the rope can be more difficult than even the trickiest climb."

DESERT SKY ZIP LINE The newest addition to the Miraval challenge family, the zip line gives guests a hawk's eye view of the gorgeous desert landscapes. "Some people assume there will be steps to the top," says Neil, "and they're shocked to get out and find they have to climb 45 feet up a pole to reach the platform where the zip line starts. So you really have two challenges—the climb and then the moment of release when you step off the platform."

GIANT'S LADDER By far the most physically demanding challenge, Giant's Ladder is precisely what it sounds like—an oversized rope ladder with rungs located five to six feet apart. Guests climb in groups, helping to pull and push each other along the way, and testing their strategic skills as well as their muscular strength. "Some people think they can climb on their own," says Neil, "but this challenge is designed to remind you that humans are social animals, and this sometimes means depending on other people. We can accomplish things in groups that we could never do alone."

FACE-TO-FACE Guests are paired up to transverse a cable network extended high into the air, and you must literally lean on the other person, using their body as a counterweight to your own, in order to proceed. "It's often easier if you're partnered with a stranger," says Neil, "because you don't drag a whole past history along with you into the challenge. But if people want to go try Face-to-Face with a spouse or partner, I always say it's better than marriage counseling. It immediately shows you the dynamic of your relationship—maybe the husband is overly protective and wants to lead the activity and help his wife, or maybe they're a very verbal couple who have to process everything before they make a move. The challenge then becomes to see if they can do it a different way. The more passive partner can take the lead, or a couple might realize that they can work well together without speaking, which might give them confidence to rely more on their nonverbal communication once they get home."

DESERT TIGHTROPE A cable is extended 35 feet in the air with periodically spaced hanging ropes to help guests work their way across the expanse from one platform to another. "The interesting thing is that there are all kinds of ways to use the ropes to help you balance and get across," says Neil. "For some people it's a very smooth trip, while others freeze halfway through with no idea what their next move should be. Desert Tightrope is a great exercise in decision making and in seeing that there's never just one perfect solution to a problem."

OUT ON A LIMB "This is one of the most deceptive challenges," Neil says. "The beam you walk across is about ten inches wide, which is plenty of room to accommodate a person's foot width, and if you just put it down on the floor, anybody could walk across it without thinking twice. Of course, if you put that same beam 25 feet in the air, it can be hard to take that first step." Neil still thinks Out on a Limb is a good first challenge for neophytes since "it's a great introduction into how the mind can turn a relatively simple task into something scary. When people make it across the beam, they often see other areas in which their perceived fears are holding them back."

WHAT WE CAN LEARN from CHALLENGES

One of the interesting things about the challenges is that the people who thrive and those who struggle might not fall along the lines you'd expect. Gender and age are rarely a factor. "Women may be more at ease than men, and someone can do their first challenge at the age of 70—it doesn't matter," says Neil. "They may get out there and have

less trouble than a 20-year-old. The people who often have the easiest time are those who have gone through something like cancer or a severe degree of trauma. For them, the stress of walking across a tightrope is actually pretty minor."

Who struggles the most? Neil says it's often those who are determined to do it "right" and do it

"well," since they're actually battling two fears: the fear of the challenge and the even more powerful fear of failure. "I always tell them that the fact they're down there at all is the most important thing," says Neil. "A large percentage of the people who come to Miraval never do a challenge—they either don't sign up or they're a no-show. So it's a big

SPA
Naga

It may be time to take your Thai massage practice a little deeper.

Thai massage is nothing like your typical massage where you lie naked on a table and are rubbed with lotions and oils. In Thai massage, the client wears loose, comfortable clothing and reclines on a large mat while the therapist helps him to stretch, frequently using the weight of his own body to assist the client in achieving a deeper position than he would have been able to reach on his own. Sometimes known tongue in cheek as "lazy man's yoga," Thai massage provides both the physical benefits of stretching and the spiritual benefits of profound meditative relaxation.

But some people have trouble relaxing into the stretches, and Thai massage can be exhausting for the therapists, who are constantly using their own strength to move the client from one position to the next. To address these issues, some forms of Thai massage use ropes to help the therapist support both his weight and the weight of the client, but this adaptation brought problems of its own. The ropes often chafed the skin of both the therapist and client, and the apparatus used was far too utilitarian to offer any spa-like aesthetic appeal. So Miraval massage therapists developed a variation that is more appealing to the senses and easier on the flesh. The treatment is known as Naga, named in honor of the half-human, half-serpent who watched over the young Buddha.

When you first show up for your appointment, you may think you've mistakenly come to audition for the Cirque du Soleil. But the large silken cloths in beautiful colors that are hanging from the ceiling are there for the therapist to use, not you. You'll lie down on a lush mat and then be moved through the sequence of classic Thai massage stretches, but since the therapists entwine themselves with the cloths to the degree they're almost suspended off the ground, this frees them to use their bodies in more creative and advanced ways.

For example, they can lightly walk on you, using the full plane of their foot as a pressure point. This is especially helpful when working on the hips and thighs, places where many clients hold tension, but which are notoriously hard muscle groups to reach because they are deep within the body and the muscles are layered. When the therapist can use the suspension cloths to control the amount of weight he is placing on the client, he can manipulate all those layers of muscles, especially the hard-to-reach ones. In other poses, the cloth almost becomes an extension of the therapist's body, a silken third arm to wrap and support the client, allowing him to sink into a deeper stretch.

The result? A massage that is deeply meditative, almost to point of being trance-like and which also provides all of the muscular and joint benefits of stretching. The fact that it looks and feels like a beautiful ballet is just a bonus.

AT HOME: While Naga is exclusive to Miraval, it is based on traditional Thai massage techniques. To find a Thai massage therapist in your area visit www.thaibodywork.com.

time to actually face the challenge, create a distraction-free zone. One of the reasons that people are often prompted to try new things at Miraval is that they're away from the worries and responsibilities of their everyday lives and all those routines that can numb us out and sap our confidence. When committing to a big goal, it's also important to divide the task into small steps. You don't climb a whole mountain in a day; you just try to make it to base camp.

"When people stand at the bottom of Giant's Ladder and look up, they're usually overwhelmed," says Neil. "It doesn't look possible. But once they start climbing, they're focused on each rung at a time or even on each separate movement it will take to get from one rung to the next. The same thing on the tightrope or when climbing the pole for the zip line or Quantum Leap. If you're in the middle of a challenge and you look down or up or across the wire at the whole space you're

about to travel, it can make you freeze. But when you stay focused on that one next step, even if it's a couple of inches, eventually you will cover the whole distance. It's a powerful lesson for life."

Finally, outcome. Remember Neil's advice that a challenge without reflection is just an isolated adrenaline rush—it will fade before you finish taking your shower. The real benefit of challenge is that pushing your limits in one area often transfers into increased confidence in other arenas of your life. You think, *If I can walk a tightrope, why would I be afraid of public speaking?* or *If I'm smart enough to figure a way to climb an unclimbable ladder, I can handle that new job.*

Besides, facing challenges gets easier over time, and eventually exploring your limits can become not scary, but fun. "I think the happiest people are those who learn to not just tolerate but actually enjoy challenge," says Neil. "Uncertainty is an inevitable part of life, and we all have to take a risk at some time or another. Learning to face challenges is just one more skill that will help you have a rich, full life."

EXERCISE
Zen Boot Camp

Along with R.I.P.P.E.D., which you'll learn about in the August chapter, Zen Boot Camp is one of the most challenging workouts offered by Miraval's Bodymindfulness Center. The class takes place outside, on the edge of the beautiful Sonoran Desert, and the chance to enjoy nature provides the Zen—the rest is pure boot camp. Sprints where you run or race-walk are interspersed with resistance work using your own body weight. Push-ups, crunches, lunges, squats, jumping jacks . . . yep, they're all there, and you move between segments quickly. This is your high-school gym class on steroids.

"Zen Boot Camp is proof that you can do an intense, sweaty, calorie-burning workout anywhere, anytime, and with no equipment," says Pam Trudeau, director of the Bodymindfulness Center. "For stamina and strength building, nothing is more effective than old-fashioned drills using jumping jacks and squats. Guests can modify the moves and go at different paces, but Zen Boot Camp always ends up being a challenging workout for everybody involved, no matter what their fitness level."

KEY POINTS FOR JULY

✿ Challenges, whether physical or mental, take you out of your day-to-day norm and thus don't merely invite you to be mindful—they compel you to be.

✿ Many challenges can only be met through teamwork and, if done in tandem with a loved one, are a great opportunity to evaluate, strengthen, and perhaps even alter the dynamics of that relationship.

✿ A fear of losing control can keep you in your comfort zone. Releasing control can take you to new insights and expand your self-definition.

NEIL MCLEOD

Neil is a professional outdoor guide and instructor whose leadership and management have been developed through his ownership of a whitewater-rafting company, his experiences as an instructor and course director for Outward Bound

Wilderness in Utah, and his involvement in the Outdoor Adventure Department at Miraval. Neil became interested in human interaction with the wilderness in his early years growing up in British Columbia; he now brings more than 18 years of experience to the Miraval Hiking, Mountain Biking, Climbing, and Challenge Course operations.

BUFFALO CARPACCIO with ARUGULA SALAD

What better way to challenge yourself in the kitchen than with a dish we can almost guarantee you've never made before? Not a lot of people eat buffalo, but Miraval Chef Justin Macy thinks that's just because they haven't tried it yet. "It's a great alternative to beef," he says. "Lower in calories and fat and full of flavor."

Not every neighborhood grocery carries buffalo, but you can always hunt your own—by using Google, that is, to help you find one of the many online purveyors of unusual meats like ostrich, rabbit, and buffalo. "And since some people get a little nervous around unfamiliar dishes," Justin advises, "it may be best to introduce it to them as an appetizer instead of an entrée."

Serve the buffalo raw—another new culinary sensation for some—and thin sliced over a salad of arugula tossed with extra-virgin olive oil, balsamic vinegar, lemon, capers, and Parmigiano-Reggiano cheese. It's perfect for a hot summer day and fiendishly simple to make, but we guarantee you that none of your dinner guests will ever call you boring.

MAKES 4 SERVINGS

4 oz. buffalo tenderloin, trimmed of all fat

1 Tbsp. Parmigiano-Reggiano cheese

2 tsp. capers

1 Tbsp. sun-dried tomatoes, chopped

2 tsp. fresh lemon segments

1 c. arugula

1 Tbsp. balsamic vinegar

1 Tbsp. extra-virgin olive oil

Freeze buffalo tenderloin until completely frozen solid, about 24 hours. Use a very sharp carving knife or deli slicer to cut the tenderloin into slices and overlap them on a small square of parchment paper in a circular pattern. Repeat three more times to complete all four servings.

Using a vegetable peeler, peel small strips off of the cheese wedge.

Drain capers, and chop the sun-dried tomatoes.

Cut lemon into slices, and then cut into small sections.

In a small mixing bowl, combine arugula greens, olive oil, and balsamic vinegar.

Place one chilled plate at a time upside down over one of the parchment sheets with the shaved tenderloin and then flip over, gently pressing parchment against plate. Slowly remove parchment from tenderloin slices. Arrange arugula greens in the middle of the plate and make small piles of the cheese, capers, sun-dried tomatoes, and lemon. Repeat with the other three plates. Serve immediately.

CALORIES: 49; TOTAL FAT: 1 G; CARBOHYDRATES: 2 G; DIETARY FIBER: 0 G; PROTEIN: 7 G

OBSTACLES

August

OVERCOMING OBSTACLES Difficulties, challenges, setbacks . . . whatever you want to call it, trouble is part of life. And it isn't just you. The greatest spiritual leaders of all time, from Jesus to Buddha, certainly encountered temptation and doubt along the way. In fact, how we respond to the obstacles in our lives may be the greatest test of how far we've truly come in our journey of self-awareness. If handled correctly, resistance—whether it comes in the form of weights in the gym or painful memories—only offers us the chance to ultimately grow stronger.

HEALING PAST TRAUMA and SETTING YOUR SPIRIT FREE to SOAR

[EXPERT] *Tim Frank, N.M.D.*

SPIRIT FLIGHT WAS NAMED BEST SPA TREATMENT BY *SPAFINDER* TWO YEARS IN A ROW—WHICH IS SLIGHTLY IRONIC SINCE, WHILE HE IS HAPPY FOR THE ACCOLADES, ITS CREATOR DR. TIM FRANK, N.M.D., DOESN'T REALLY THINK OF IT AS A SPA TREATMENT. "I CONSIDER SPIRIT FLIGHT A CEREMONY," SAYS DR. TIM, WHO COMBINES DEEP TISSUE AND STRUCTURAL MASSAGE WITH ACUPUNCTURE, CRANIAL SACRAL THERAPY, SPINAL ALIGNMENT, SHAMANISM, AND NATIVE AMERICAN RITUALS TO CREATE A HEALING EXPERIENCE LIKE NO OTHER.

"Conventional medicine often strives to suppress the symptoms of disease, but I believe in the concept of *Tolle causem,* which means *Treat the cause,*" says Dr. Tim. "If dis-eases of the mind and spirit, many of which were caused by past trauma, are not healed, they will manifest as discomfort, dysfunction, or physical illness. Symptoms can be beneficial because they show us where we've experienced spiritual wounding." Dr. Tim uses three primary tools in his work with clients at Miraval: Holographic Memory Resolution (HMR), Spirit Flight, and the Samadhi Healing Ceremony. The three therapies are all the result of Dr. Tim's broad and varied studies in psychology,

medicine, energy work, and spiritual healing.

The son of an intuitive healer, Dr. Tim says he was "putting hands on people" by the time he was nine. While his father and brother were going to football games, young Tim was at home "learning healing techniques from my mother, who was part of the New Age community of Boulder, Colorado. There was always some sort of spiritual ceremony going on in my house, and my mother worked with practitioners from all over the world." The Native American piece of the puzzle comes through his Cherokee godfather who brought Tim to his reservation to study shamanic energy work. And the Asian

modalities are the result of time Tim spent in Japan as an undergraduate student in psychology. "I wound up in a Zen Buddhist monastery," he says, "and while I was there I went through an earthquake, got pneumonia, broke my ankle, and suffered the worst heartbreak of my life. Finally the Zen master looked at me and said, 'Go home or die.'"

Knowing he was meant to be a healer but unsure of exactly what form this calling would take, Tim enrolled in naturopathic medical school. "But at the same time I was practicing Western medicine," he says, "I was also still traveling around doing spiritual healings with my godfather. When my mother and godfather died, I feared their traditions would die with them. So I told myself I would devote myself to healing ceremonies for three years in tribute to them."

Seven years later, Dr. Tim says, "I can still put on the white coat and write a prescription for an antibiotic or an antidepressant when they're needed. There's a time and place for those things. But the vast majority of my work is ceremonial, using shamanistic and bodywork modalities. I'm not afraid to say the words *God* or *miracle* because healing, in many cases, must take place on a spiritual level before it can cure whatever is manifesting on a physical level. With these healing ceremonies, I am not afraid to say *God, divine intervention,* or *miracles,* because I have no other way to explain the healings that occur . . . nor would I."

THE SPIRIT FLIGHT CEREMONY

Dr. Tim's signature therapy is the Spirit Flight, in which he combines elements of everything he's learned in his studies around the world, from acupuncture to shamanism to prayer, all aimed at restoring balance and peace.

"Spirit Flight is like pushing a reboot button on the hard drive of your body and soul," he says. "In the journey of life we get so caught up in our responsibilities and the roles we play that we forget who we really are. We lose touch with our divine purpose." This dissatisfaction can bubble along undetected in the subconscious for years, but at pivotal times in our life, certain key transition points, the dissatisfaction can no longer be held back. It gushes forward and manifests itself as either a physical ailment, depression, anxiety, or an addiction.

The Spirit Flight actually begins before it begins. Each morning Dr. Tim is given a list of the clients he'll be seeing that day, and he goes alone to his treatment room for a half hour of prayer and meditation before he meets the first person on the schedule. "I ask that I will have the spiritual guidance needed to facilitate their healing," he says, "and I also pray that they will be open to it, that the people coming into this space are ready to make changes in their life. Because this isn't a one-way street, it's a contract between the two of us. If what you want is a great massage, you can walk down the sidewalk to the spa and get one of the best massages in the country. But this is a ceremony, not a treatment, and the client needs to be prepared for the journey."

When the client shows up—usually nervous, since Spirit Flight has an oft-repeated reputation for being intense—Dr. Tim begins with a conversation to clarify the issues he or she would like to work on. "With each person who comes through the door, I look for their deepest point of wounding," he says. "After we've introduced ourselves and they've taken a seat, I purify the room. I smudge with sweetgrass sage, whisk the air with feathers, and use fire in a shell to pass a cleansing flame over the bed where we'll be working. It's essential that I cleanse the room, the table, myself, and any bad energies they brought in with them because every religion on Earth sanctifies the holy ground before they begin their rituals.

"Understanding that what is about to happen is a ritual makes it easier for people to let go and trust in the process," says Dr. Tim. "We are a culture that has lost ceremony. Yes, we have weddings, baptisms, bar pleading for a want or need to be fulfilled, but it is rather like a ripple in a pond, allowing serenity and grace to guide you on. Somehow this experience instills in the nervous system a frame of reference—a neural pathway, if you will, to be safe, nurtured, and embodied in a calming confidence/worthiness of one's divine consciousness. Now, if people, places, or events of negativity arise, the nervous system can draw from this new frame of reference and respond to the stimulus that is in front of it—in the *present*—as opposed to the hairpin trigger of the pain, self-esteem issues, or projection of the past. Thus, one can respond appropriately with the proper amount of emotion and response for today.

THE SPIRITUAL CYCLES of LIFE

While Spirit Flight can be helpful at any age, there are certain points in our life cycle when the "urge to purge" is especially strong. "It's like we only have a certain amount of RAM on the hard drive," Dr. Tim says. "And every 27 to 29 years we need to clear it out and start over. The first time it happens we're young adults and often don't have the maturity or insight to respond to the challenge in a thoughtful way."

Dr. Tim points out how many major life decisions—including marriage and the birth of a first child—we often make during the ages of 27 and 29. "All of us are burned somehow as children," he says. "We all emerge from childhood with some issues of self-esteem or trauma. And the decisions made in the first cycle are often influenced by them. A woman with unresolved father images marries a man who treats her just like daddy did. A

man who had an unreliable, alcoholic mother winds up working for an unreliable, alcoholic boss. Something about the situation may feel familiar, and this is our first chance to recognize a pattern from our childhood and respond in a different way. But most of us miss the chance this first time through. When we feel the pain we medicate, medicate, medicate . . . and some people choose to check out at this point. If you look at the long list of stars who died young, people like Amy Winehouse who were incredibly talented but incredibly troubled, you see that a high percentage of the ones who committed suicide or overdosed did so around the ages of 27 to 29."

By the time the cycle comes through again you're 54 to 58. You're in what society often calls a "midlife crisis" and Dr. Tim calls "a second chance for self-examination. It's

another opportunity to define who you were really put on Earth to be, to do it all over again but this time with more wisdom."

This doesn't mean the process is pretty. "A lot of skeletons come out of the closet when people reach their 50s," says Dr. Tim. "Children are leaving home, which may bring feelings of loss and grief. People are often experiencing their first serious health problems or noticing that they don't bounce back from small injuries and illnesses as quickly as they once could. Marriages come under pressure or fail completely. People often feel like their world is turning upside down, and this sort of crisis can push you either way. An alcoholic who managed to stay sober for 20 years finds himself waking up in Vegas with a hooker. So many times I see a woman sitting before me sobbing and when I ask her how old

MEDITATION
Overcoming Obstacles

Challenges can be a gift. If we look at the journeys of heroes, whether they're legends from myth or the lives of people we admire from history, their stories are always full of obstacles. As long as we don't engage with them personally, these challenges can become vital stepping-stones on the path to our personal truth.

The problem is that most of us engage. We spring up to fight whatever life circumstance we see as a problem and thus are unable to hear any message it's intended to deliver. But spiritual tradition shows us that whatever we resist, expands. The more we obsess, the more power the problem has over us, and the more it limits our capacity of joy. The potential gift becomes a source of sorrow.

The following short meditation is designed to help us reduce our emotional attachment to our problems and is thus the first step in stopping our need to fight them and opening our hearts to learning the lessons they have come to teach us. It can be done on a regular basis or anytime you sense yourself becoming overwhelmed with negativity or obsessing about a particular situation in your life.

Sit quietly and take a few slow breaths to calm yourself. Briefly scan your body for held tension, and if you find any signs of it, such as discomfort in your abdomen, a headache, or clinched fists, gently send an intention of release and healing to that part of your body.

Picture yourself seated beside a gentle, slow-moving stream. It is a beautiful day, and the trees above you provide a canopy of shade. Gaze down into the stream, and watch leaves go by. The leaves represent circumstances of your life, for good or bad. Notice how they each float away in time. New leaves come, and then they pass by as well. Life is like this. Events will come and then go. It is not your job to stop their progress. Simply observe the passing of the leaves without judgment.

Another variation of this visualization is to imagine yourself holding the strings of a group of balloons. Each balloon represents one of your worries, some circumstance you cannot control or a person who has upset you. One at a time, release each balloon. Look up and watch it rise above you, carried away by the wind until it is out of sight. Release each balloon, one at a time, until your hands are empty.

When your visualization is complete, repeat an affirmation in your mind. You can affirm anything you wish, but it should be stated in the present tense and use positive language. In other words, rather than saying, "Someday when all this is behind me, I hope I can learn to be calm again," or "After the surgery, maybe I'll feel better," simply say, "I am calm," or "I am healthy."

End your meditation with an affirmative statement of whatever quality you wish to bring into your life. Gradually allow your breath to deepen and slowly bring movement back into your body.

SPA
Detoxifying Botanical Body Wrap

There are many ways to release toxicity, and one of them is through the skin. Body wraps, which involve being lightly swaddled in warm comforting layers of cloth, encourage purifying perspiration and also prepare the skin to replenish itself with moisture.

The Miraval Detoxifying Botanical Body Wrap, developed in conjunction with Clarins USA, is a 75-minute treatment that helps to release impurities while improving your skin's elasticity and tone with a pampering plant-based body wrap. The treatment begins with a light application of botanical body oil, followed by a gentle dry brushing to remove dead skin cells. Next, your whole body is treated with a mask of detoxifying white clay, which is enhanced with an antioxidant-rich blend of red raspberries and cranberries.

While you rest on the table, lightly wrapped in a cocoon of warmed towels, your therapist will massage your scalp, encouraging you to drift further into relaxation. After a refreshing shower with a botanical cleansing gel, a contouring body mask is applied to seal in the moisture and sustain your youthful new glow.

The Botanical Power Detoxifying Body Wrap is a luxurious and aromatic therapeutic body treatment, similar to our Miraval Detoxifying Botanical Body Wrap, that will help detoxify your skin of toxins and impurities while nourishing and rehydrating, and can be done at home with a little advanced preparation. A great change-of-seasons body renewal to enliven the mind and body!

HOME CARE: For the detoxifying clay, obtain small quantities (approximately 1/4 cup each) of freeze-dried cranberries and raspberries, white clay, oatmeal, and rice powder at your local health-food store. Place the freeze-dried berries and oatmeal in a coffee grinder or small food processor and pulse until a fine powder. Combine this with the rice powder in a bowl, and add enough hot water to make a creamy mixture. Then add a dash of your favorite oil (almond, coconut, grapeseed, or jojoba) or Clarins Anti-Eau Body Oil.

Before applying the berry-clay mixture, you will want to increase the circulation in the skin by doing a dry brushing on lightly oiled skin, with light upward strokes toward the heart/lymph nodes (elbow to shoulder, wrist to elbow, and so on). Apply the clay and wrap up in a cotton sheet to stay warm. Try to keep the clay on for at least 15 minutes for maximum benefits. Rinse off and apply your favorite body butter or Clarins Satin Smooth body lotion to rehydrate.

---

she is, she'll answer, 'I'm 55,' and I think, *Of course you are.*"

But if you know you're on the cusp of this cycle, you have a chance to prepare and thus modify the effects of the change. One of the best things you can do as you approach midlife is identify your issues before they come up and get the tools in your toolbox ready to deal with them. That can mean therapy, energy work, or coming to a place like Miraval. Of course, any kind of change brings disruption, and you can't prepare so thoroughly that you'll avoid all of the emotions—not that you would even want to if you could. "But if you've done the work to recognize and name your issues," says Dr. Tim, "they don't bowl you over with the same kind of power. You just say, 'Oh, here's my daddy stuff coming up again.'"

HOLOGRAPHIC MEMORY RESOLUTION

Along with therapist and teacher Brent Baum, Dr. Tim offers another type of healing called Holographic Memory Resolution (HMR). HMR is built around the awareness that not only do our minds hold on to hurt and fear from the past, but that these negative memories can imprint into our bodies as well.

One of the most interesting things about the mind-body connection is that our bodies react much the same way to a visualization or memory as they do to events happening in real time. This quality works in our favor in many situations, such as being able to relax during meditation by imagining ourselves on a pleasant beach instead of in our not-so-pleasant office cubicle. Athletes can virtually train by going through their routines in their minds, and any of us can use visualization to prepare for an upcoming event, whether it's a business presentation or childbirth. But, on the flip side, negative memories can keep retraumatizing our minds and retriggering our bodies. We've all had the experience of an event so upsetting that just recalling it can activate physical responses. The danger may be far away, separated from our present

reality by miles and years, but when we remember it, our body still feels the fear. Our heart beats faster, we become light-headed with anxiety, our stomachs twist, and our breathing gets shallow.

There's a way out of this cycle of being continually retraumatized by past events, and it's HMR. The process can help clients reframe trauma in a way that will no longer trigger the same emotional response; speaking in the most simple of terms, HMR gives you the chance to eject an old memory tape and replace it with a new one.

To better understand how HMR works, let's look at the example of a woman in her 40s who came to Miraval primarily because she wanted to lose weight. This woman, whom we can call Beth for purposes of our example, knew that she was an emotional eater who would reach for certain comfort foods whenever she was stressed. But she didn't know why. Beth suspected the reason might lie with her controlling, critical mother, so she booked a session with Dr. Tim to see if she could recover more specific memories.

The HMR session began with Dr. Tim putting his left hand at the base of her neck. Placing your

hand on someone here is classically comforting, which is why so many people rub their own necks when they're stressed, but pressure on the C7 vertebra also stimulates a parasympathetic response. "We operate about 5 percent out of our conscious minds and 95 percent from the subconscious," says Dr. Tim. "Before you can heal a memory you have to access the part of the subconscious where the trauma has been stored."

Dr. Tim then asked Beth where the memory was located and what sort of qualities it had in terms of shape, size, color, or texture. "Each emotion manifests in a very specific way," says Dr. Tim. "I've heard people describe their feelings as burning, spiky, shiny . . . all sorts of adjectives." With Dr. Tim prompting her to provide increasing levels of detail, Beth was able to describe her emotion as a black, doughnut-shaped disk, which was lodged in her throat and made her feel as if she were choking. From there Dr. Tim asked her how young she was when this feeling first manifested in her body. Beth remembered being four years old and in the hall of her childhood home, outside her baby brother's room.

PRICKLY PEAR BARBECUE-GLAZED PORK TENDERLOIN with GRILLED WATERMELON

When it comes to healthy eating, sometimes the biggest obstacle we have to overcome is our craving for comfort food. For example, what's August without a backyard barbecue—and what's barbecue except an unholy trinity of fat, sugar, and salt?

Miraval's culinary team has come to the rescue with a full-flavored pork tenderloin that's perfect for a classic summer cookout. Served with the sinfully sweet grilled watermelon and fresh broccolini, this is a lean and flavorful way to celebrate the waning days of summer.

MAKES 4 SERVINGS

16 oz. pork tenderloin, trimmed of fat

Prickly Pear Barbecue Sauce *(see recipe)*

4 slices watermelon (approximately 1 cup)

2 Tbsp. agave nectar

2 c. fresh steamed broccolini

Kosher salt to taste

Black pepper to taste

Cut a 2-inch-thick slice of watermelon, then cut it into four 2-ounce wedges. Brush watermelon on both sides with agave nectar.

Lightly season pork tenderloin with salt and pepper.

Place pork on hot grill and mark on all sides; cook to internal temperature of medium (140°F), about 8 minutes, while brushing lightly with barbecue sauce and rotating. The sauce will caramelize onto the meat during this time.

Place agave-coated watermelon slices on grill and mark on both sides to caramelize; they should have dark grill marks, almost burned.

Paint a stripe of barbecue sauce across each plate.

Remove pork and watermelon from grill. Place a piece of watermelon on top of the barbecue sauce stripe. Slice the pork tenderloin on a bias crosswise, and arrange the slices over the watermelon. Serve with a ½ cup of fresh steamed broccolini.

PRICKLY PEAR BARBECUE SAUCE
MAKES 2 CUPS; SERVINGS: 32; SERVING SIZE: 1 TABLESPOON

1 c. ketchup

¼ c. apple cider vinegar

1 c. prickly pear syrup

2 Tbsp. agave syrup

2 Tbsp. molasses

¼ c. blackening spice mix

Combine all ingredients in a heavy-bottomed sauce pot and simmer over medium heat until sauce is thick enough to coat the back of a spoon.

Refrigerate until ready to use, up to 1 week. Note: Agave syrup or honey may be substituted for the prickly pear syrup.

CALORIES: 220; TOTAL FAT: 2 G; CARBOHYDRATES: 25 G; DIETARY FIBER: 2 G; PROTEIN: 26 G

September

HARVEST Food is an enormous part of our lives—not just as nourishment and fuel for our bodies, but as a source of comfort, pleasure, and celebration. Even if we're committed to losing weight and eating in a more health-conscious way, this doesn't mean that we don't still deserve all of the joys that a good meal can bring.

to encourage guests to get better at ascertaining where they are on the hunger scale. If you pause at regular intervals throughout the day and check in with yourself, you may recognize that you're not really hungry at all and that something else, like boredom or anxiety, is making you think it's time to eat. If you're at the point of slight hunger, eat a few walnuts or a piece of fruit. If you're feeling significant hunger, it's time for a meal. And if you're at the point of shaky, queasy, headachy hunger, you've waited too long. Just taking a minute to access and acknowledge where you are on the scale can save you from a lot of mindless gobbling.

You can employ the same "checking in" exercise throughout the course of a meal. As we've noted, it takes 20 minutes for the body to recognize satiety, so if you're eating too fast or eating mindlessly, you probably will miss the early signals of "almost enough." At different points in the meal, it's smart to pause and ask yourself, *Where am I on the hunger scale?* Gradually, you'll begin to ascertain what "almost enough," "a little too full," or "whoa, I ate way too much" feel like for you.

SPA
Bountiful Earth

Bountiful Earth is a Miraval exclusive, a luxuriant 100-minute treatment that takes place in one of the resort's outdoor-treatment rooms. As the name implies, the Bountiful Earth circles the globe for inspiration, bringing in a variety of products from all over the world, carefully blended to appeal to your senses and nourish your body.

The journey begins in Northern Africa with a cleansing scrub using a loofah and Moroccan Rose body wash. Asia is represented with a vigorous skin exfoliation using bamboo, ginger grass, and mineral-rich silt to leave your skin refreshed and glowing. Then we travel across the Pacific to Mexico, soothing your body with a Yucatan-inspired Coco-Mole clay wrap, which really does smell good enough to eat. While you're relaxing into the warm wrap, you'll receive a face and scalp massage. And our journey ends where it begins, in the rustic mountains of the American Southwest. You'll be led outside to wash off the remnants of your clay body mask in your private shower, using cleansers scented with cedarwood and juniper. Finally you return to the table for a full-body massage using lime silk oil with citrus hints and juniper-cedarwood body butter.

This treatment not only takes you around the world with smells and sensations but also combines three of the best spa treatments at Miraval: a scrub, a wrap, and a massage. You'll leave relaxed and fresh, with your skin soft and subtly scented.

BUTTERNUT SQUASH RISOTTO

People are always impressed when you make risotto, but the dish isn't technically as hard as everyone thinks. Admittedly it is a little time intensive—so just be prepared to keep stirring!

The roasted butternut squash in the following recipe is a nod to the fact that fall is coming and that we're switching from late summer vegetables to the more gourd-like produce associated with autumn. The squash also adds an almost velvety texture, smoothly hiding the absence of cream and cheese in the dish and providing the decadent "mouthfeel" of a classic risotto. And the golden rich color is divine.

½ average-size butternut squash (about one pound before cooking, about 1¾ cups after peeling)

½ tsp. garlic, minced

2 Tbsp. yellow onion, chopped

¼ tsp. Miraval Oil Blend (3:1 mix canola oil and extra-virgin olive oil)

1 cup arborio or carnaroli rice, dry

4 cups hot vegetable stock

3 Tbsp. chardonnay wine

¼ cup cooked quinoa

½ tsp. fresh oregano, chopped

½ tsp. fresh thyme leaves

1 tsp. kosher salt

¼ tsp. ground black pepper

¼ tsp. nutmeg, optional

Preheat oven to 400°F; cut squash in half lengthwise and scoop out the seeds, place squash facedown on a cookie sheet, and add just enough water to cover the bottom of the pan. Roast the squash until the skin begins to blister and the squash is soft, about 35 minutes. Allow squash to cool until it can be handled comfortably.

Using a peeler or a spoon, remove the skin and medium dice the squash.

Sauté onions and garlic in Miraval Oil Blend until translucent and aromas are released, about 1 minute.

Add the dry rice and continue to sauté until the rice is lightly browned, about 1 minute.

Add butternut squash and sauté for 45 seconds.

Deglaze the pan with the wine, and continue cooking over low heat until the liquid is mostly evaporated, about 20 seconds.

Add the heated vegetable stock a half cup at a time, stirring often until the liquid is almost evaporated before adding the next batch, until the rice is cooked, about 35 minutes.

Remove from heat, stir in the cooked quinoa and herbs. Season to taste with salt, pepper, and nutmeg if desired.

CALORIES: 144; TOTAL FAT: TRACE; CARBOHYDRATE: 32G; PROTEIN: 3G; SODIUM: 28MG; DIETARY FIBER: 3G

October

BALANCE "Life in Balance" has been a phrase deeply connected to Miraval since the resort debuted in 1995. The May 2012 opening of the new Life in Balance Spa is only the latest illustration of how central the concept of balance is to everything that happens at Miraval. But our definition of balance is not stillness and immobility. Instead, it is acknowledging all of the components that come together to create a full and dynamic life: solitude and companionship, activity and rest, shade and sunshine, the comfort of tradition and the stimulation of new experiences. The goal of a life in balance is not to get all of the moving parts of our lives to stop; it's to learn to appreciate the dance.

VEGETARIAN BLACK BEAN SOUP

Shorter days. Falling leaves. Crisper air. Pumpkins on the stoop, and the roar of a crowd at a football game. No dish goes better with the feeling of autumn than a piping hot bowl of soup. The recipe below is hearty, satisfying, and a Miraval staple. The peppers, cumin, and cayenne team up to provide a kick of flavor; and the dish is easy to make and full of plant protein and fiber. Remember how Junelle Lupiani suggested we eat beans every day? This black bean soup is a simple and delicious way to meet that directive.

YIELDS ABOUT 1 QT.; MAKES 8 SERVINGS; SERVING SIZE: ½ CUP

¾ c. raw black beans, cleaned and sorted

2 tsp. Miraval Oil Blend (3:1 mix of canola oil and extra-virgin olive oil)

½ c. yellow onion, diced

1½ tsp. garlic, chopped fine

¼ c. red bell pepper, diced

¼ c. Anaheim or poblano chili, diced

½ Tbsp. cumin powder

½ Tbsp. dried oregano

1 bay leaf

¼ tsp. kosher or sea salt

½ Tbsp. ground black pepper

⅛ tsp. cayenne pepper

1 Tbsp. fresh parsley, chopped fine

2 Tbsp. cilantro, rinsed and chopped

1 qt. plus 1 cup vegetable stock

1 Tbsp. dry sherry wine

½ Tbsp. brown sugar

1 Tbsp. fresh lemon juice

Soak beans overnight, covering with enough water to keep all beans completely soaked. Then drain beans and discard soaking liquid.

Preheat a large heavy-duty pot; add Miraval Oil Blend.

Sauté onion, garlic, red bell pepper, and Anaheim or poblano chili until onions begin to become translucent. Stir in cumin, oregano, bay leaf, salt, black pepper, cayenne, parsley, and cilantro. Add stock and bring to a boil. Reduce heat and cook uncovered until beans are tender and soup is reduced by about half, about 45 minutes.

Add sherry, brown sugar, and lemon juice to the soup. Simmer 10 minutes, stirring frequently. Discard bay leaf. Adjust seasoning if needed.

SERVING SUGGESTIONS Top with a teaspoon of sour cream or plain yogurt, sliced jalapeños, and cumin-scented tortilla strips. To make tortilla strips, cut three corn tortillas into thin, ½-inch strips. Place in a mixing bowl, spray lightly with ½ tsp. oil, and toss in a pinch of ground cumin and kosher salt. Lay out on a cookie sheet, and bake at 400°F until crisp and fragrant, about 5 minutes.

CALORIES: 128; TOTAL FAT: 3 G; CARBOHYDRATES: 21 G; DIETARY FIBER: 7 G; PROTEIN: 5 G

TUDE
November

GRATITUDE "If the only prayer you ever say in your whole life is 'thank you,' that would suffice." These words by the German philosopher Meister Eckhart remind us of the profound power of gratitude and why it is at the center of almost all forms of spiritual practice. The ability to experience and express gratitude opens the heart, and more surprisingly, even the brain, since it reorders the patterns in which our neurons fire, directing them to more automatically seek positive emotions. Gratitude also connects us to other people and to the wider world of nature, gently but persistently reminding us that we are all part of a broad web of energy and life. No one can feel grateful and still feel alone.

Nature helps us reboot, so one of the simplest ways to reconnect with the joy-based parts of our brain is to spend time outdoors. "Just a short walk outside can have a healing effect if we're fully connected to the sensory experiences," says Pam. "The colors, the textures, the smells, and the sounds will stimulate our energy centers. Remember how earlier we spoke of gratitude as being a sense of interconnectedness and seeing that we're part of a larger whole? Nothing connects us to that wider world faster or more pleasurably than spending time in nature. In a vibrational sense, we become attuned with the plants, the sun, and the animals—and they

remind our body of its own innate intelligence and ability to heal. In nature, everything has a vibration that encourages the human body to be vibrant, so it counterbalances the pressure of modern life, where we are often surrounded by unnatural vibrations: electrical appliances, computers, cell phones, televisions, social media. We're around beeping, ringing, buzzing machines all day, to the degree that I recently saw a report that city birds were becoming so affected by all the cellphone noise that they're beginning to sing ringtones. All this artificial vibrational stimulation has numbed us out as a culture and left us overwhelmed. If even the birds are

confused, it's not surprising that we humans are disconnected from the more subtle energies of nature."

But time spent outside in solitude and silence can restore our equilibrium with surprising ease. If you work in a city, eating lunch in a quiet, tucked-away corner of a park can have a calming effect, and if even this sort of respite isn't available, meditations that guide you to imagine yourself in a peaceful place create many of the same benefits of actually being in that place. There's a reason why so many gratitude meditations, including the one described in this chapter, begin with a visualization of walking through a beautiful outdoor setting.

We have to consciously create chances for the body to discharge tension because most of us can't count on naturally finding them in the midst of our daily lives. To add to the problem, this constant low-grade stress is a relatively new phenomenon, and our bodies haven't yet developed skills for coping with it. Just as the brain evolved to recognize danger, it also learned how to recognize when the danger had passed. In the earlier example, once the predator was gone, either because he'd been outrun or defeated, the human

SPA
Ginger Healer

Some of the most delightful spa treatments at Miraval are those that take place in the outdoor spa village, where each individual room seems like a fantasy cabin in the woods, and the outdoor showers provide both complete privacy and the naughty sensation of running naked through the rain.

The Ginger Healer begins with a full-body massage on one of the heated tables, which is adjusted to ensure your complete comfort. The therapist will likewise adjust his or her hand pressure from a light skin-stimulating touch to a more firm deep-tissue level upon your request. Each treatment includes a pressure-point face massage, which brings an energetic tingle to your skin while also helping to relieve any discomfort from seasonal allergies. All of the lotions and oils used in the treatment are scented with the light, unobtrusive aroma of ginger, which has healing properties that have been acknowledged in cultures around the world.

After the massage, you'll enjoy a full body scrub with ginger, rosemary, and sea salt to gently remove any dead skin cells and reveal the more youthful, softer

skin beneath. Then your therapist will lead you out to your private shower—the yummiest part of the treatment for many people—to allow you to wash away the scrub. You'll return to the table for a final application of body cream and leave the village feeling smooth, refreshed, and completely relaxed. This is one of those treatments that's impossible not to like.

would relax completely, and the generated fight-or-flight hormones would leave his system. In today's world, where stress is more chronic, we have to devise ways to help our body release stored tension.

"We're contracted," Pam says. "When we hold our breath or breathe shallowly, when we don't exercise and choose to live our lives stuffed in tiny rooms and tiny cars, when we deny the emotions

we're feeling . . . the result of all this is a body in contraction, with its energies dammed up. Being in nature—walking on the earth, feeling the sun, exchanging gases with the plants around us—restarts the natural energy flow. I'm not talking about wearing headphones for music or taking a friend so you'll have someone to talk to or training for a marathon and constantly monitoring your time. It's easy to be

outside and still not notice, much less appreciate, your surroundings. I'm talking about taking some time every day to connect with the natural world and let it work its magic upon you. Our bodies crave these chances to recycle energy and purge tension. They need an energy that is greater in mass and in openness to help them do this, but it can happen with ease and grace if we put ourselves in the right environment."

INTEGRATIVE THERAPY

Integrative therapies, which are designed to activate the body, mind, and spirit simultaneously, can have the same effects of time spent in nature: releasing tension, realigning our energies, and rebooting the joy centers of our brains. In her popular Shuniya Sound sessions at Miraval, Pam uses a combination of intentional conversation; bodywork in the form of Thai massage, Chi Nei Tsang, and shiatsu; and the powerful vibrations of traditional Tibetan bowls to help guests attain a state of pure peace.

"The focus of the session is to create integration between our mind, body, and spirit," says Pam. "We do this by first becoming aware of our thought processes, then plugging into the words and emotions to help us align the mind with the heart and set the intention for the session. Vibrationally speaking, the cells of our body and our emotions are listening and getting ready to take action according to our thoughts. Then we assist the body to release old energy and make space for these new intentions through bodywork and the vibrations of the singing bowls and gongs."

The ceremony session is actually a festival of vibration. As Pam points out, two human voices in conversation create vibrations, and we automatically attune to the voices around us. If you have any doubt, simply whisper and watch the person you're in conversation with drop his own volume, too. Or consider how some voices automatically soothe and delight you—either musically or simply in conversation—while others can create an equally automatic sense of displeasure or mistrust.

With this in mind, Pam starts every session with a few minutes of conversation in which she and the client discuss what they hope to achieve. The moments of conversation give Pam and the client the chance to establish what she calls "limbic trust" through their shared voices. "The limbic part of the brain is the area that invites us to emotionally connect with each other," says Pam, and the conversation also gives her an opportunity to learn a little about the client. "We talk about what they want to bring more of into their lives," she says. "That's very important to set the tone—no pun intended—of the ceremony. I

want to help people see how the things that are worrying them are depleting their energy and simultaneously invite in more joy, love, peace, health, new opportunities . . . whatever it is. Each person has to go to the right place for them.

"People usually know when they're blocked," says Pam, "but they may not consciously know what's blocking them. My clients often tell me that they want to open up space in their lives and frequently say that the spiritual dimension of their lives has been stunted." Pam points out that women especially are often so preoccupied with nurturing others that they may find themselves totally "tapped out" at various points in their lives. They don't believe that they can find even 15 minutes in their day to walk in nature or to meditate.

The conversation also gives her a chance to zero in on areas where healing may be needed. "A client might realize she's anxious and exhausted," says Pam, "but she may not see, for example, that her anxiety is caused by a critical mind. It often jumps right out at me, just as it's probably clear to her friends and family members at home. I may say something like, 'I'm hearing a lot of self-criticism in your comments,' but I try to minimize my feedback because it's always better if clients come to these discoveries on their own. A massage therapist or practitioner can't push them into it, and it's important that I don't try to project onto them what I think they need to know. Self-realization is the first step in healing, and your own 'Aha' moment is far more powerful than anything anyone else can tell you."

Finally, Pam also uses these few minutes of talk to explore where the positive past memories may lie. "Sometimes I will ask a client to describe to me the last time they felt joy and peace," says Pam. "It's important that they describe it not just in words but that they actually re-create in themselves the feelings of that moment. I ask them to describe textures, smells, and sounds. It's easy to get lost in the tag words—words like *peacefulness* or *balance* or *love* sound pretty, but the question is, exactly what does that feel like to you? I say, 'How does peace feel in your particular body? Give me three words.'"

The idea is that clients don't merely describe and recall their last experience of peace in an abstract way—"I was walking on the beach"— but rather invoke it on sensory levels: the crunch of the sand, the soft rhythmic roar of the waves, the coconut smell of their sunscreen, the feel of hair blowing in the wind. "I encourage people to talk from the heart," says Pam, "and you can tell when they're really back there. Their breathing deepens, and their voices slow down. You can hear the actual moment when they're fully immersed in the memory. Often they say 'Ummm . . .' as if they're pausing to consider their words, but this 'ummm' is also the end sound of most mantras. So while they are searching for what to say, the act of their lips coming together in the 'ummm' sound begins to connect the heart, mind, and body."

This is the point where the ceremonial healing begins. "At that moment they're feeling expansive, and time begins to slow," Pam says. "Similar to the way mantras work, sending signals to the brain as certain areas and points are stimulated on our palate, the words we speak affect our body mentally and emotionally. The words we speak generate an action, mood, or emotion to help us have our identity in every given situation. When we speak or declare out loud what we are releasing from our being, this

PAN-SEARED DUCK with GRANNY SMITH APPLE and CHIPOTLE CHUTNEY

November means Thanksgiving, and Thanksgiving means turkey, right? Maybe not. There are times when we might want to reach beyond the standard Thanksgiving menu while still staying true to certain traditional flavors: a game bird, sweet potatoes, late-harvest apples, and that combination of smoke and spice that we all associate with the richest autumnal flavors.

MAKES 4 SERVINGS

4 four-ounce duck breasts, trimmed of fat and sinew

1 medium roasted sweet potato, peeled and sliced ½ inch thick

½ tsp. Miraval Oil Blend (3:1 mix of canola oil and extra-virgin olive oil)

⅛ tsp. kosher salt

⅛ tsp. freshly ground black pepper

½ c. Granny Smith Apple and Chipotle Chutney (see *recipe*)

Preheat the oven to 400°F.

Lightly season the duck breasts on both sides with the salt and pepper.

Heat a ¼ teaspoon of the oil in large ovenproof skillet over medium-high heat. Add the duck; sear on both sides for 1½ minutes each, turning once.

Transfer the skillet to the oven and roast for about 4 minutes, then flip the duck over and continue cooking until medium rare, about 4 more minutes.

Remove the duck from the oven and let rest in the pan for 3 minutes.

Preheat a sauté pan over high heat. Lightly season sweet-potato slices with a pinch of kosher salt and pepper and place in sauté pan with remaining oil, searing on both sides until crusty and brown, about 1½ minutes per side. Use a spatula to turn them so they don't crumble.

To serve, place the sweet-potato slices in the middle of each plate and cut the duck into thin slices on a bias. Arrange the duck slices on top of the potato, spoon 2 tablespoons of the chutney over the top of the duck, and serve.

GRANNY SMITH APPLE and CHIPOTLE CHUTNEY

**MAKES 1 CUP;
SERVING SIZE 2 TABLESPOONS**

¾ c. Granny Smith apple, peeled, seeded, cored, and chopped

2 Tbsp. dried apricot, thinly sliced

2 Tbsp. red onion, thinly sliced

2 Tbsp. packed light brown sugar

2 Tbsp. apple cider vinegar

2 Tbsp. fresh orange juice

1 tsp. minced canned chipotle chili in adobo sauce

Pinch mustard seeds

Combine all of the ingredients in a medium sauce pot and bring to a boil over high heat.

Reduce the heat to medium-low and simmer, stirring occasionally until thick and the liquid is reduced by three-quarters, about 15 minutes.

Remove from the heat and keep warm until needed, or refrigerate for up to 1 week.

CALORIES: 260; TOTAL FAT: 6 G; CARBOHYDRATES: 27 G; DIETARY FIBER: 4 G; PROTEIN: 25 G

December

CELEBRATION The entire month of December falls within what's widely known as the holiday season, a time of shopping, baking, parties, and nearly nonstop activity from Thanksgiving to New Year's. While fellowship with family and friends is important, it's equally vital to remember that we're also approaching the winter solstice, where the days grow shorter, the nights grow longer, and our souls become more introspective. Work some moments of solitude and retreat into your busy December schedule, thereby honoring both the reflective and the celebratory flavor of the season. When your spirit is receptive and open, any day can be a holiday.

Hors d'oeuvres seems like such an old-fashioned term, but what else should we call these delicious bites that people serve at parties? Forget the cheese balls and the mini-quiches; these three treats are light, delicious, sophisticated, and perfect for entertaining. And the presentations are delightful. If you serve your oysters on the half shell nestled on the recommended bed of rock salt and pink peppercorns, prepare for your guests to swoon.

OYSTERS on the HALF SHELL with MANGO-GINGER COCKTAIL SAUCE and POMEGRANATE MIGNONETTE

MAKES 4 SERVINGS; SERVING SIZE: 3 OYSTERS

12 medium West Coast oysters
4 tsp. Mango-Ginger Cocktail Sauce
4 tsp. Pomegranate Mignonette

For each plate, arrange three freshly shucked raw oysters. Serve with one teaspoon of the mango-ginger cocktail sauce and pomegranate mignonette.

For an enhanced presentation, pour a half cup of rock salt on each plate, and press the oyster shells into it. This will help to keep the shells from sliding around. The rock salt may be sprinkled with paprika or crushed pink peppercorns for additional color.

MANGO-GINGER COCKTAIL SAUCE

MAKES 1 CUP;
SERVING SIZE: 1 TABLESPOON

1 mango, yields about 1 cup
1 Tbsp. horseradish
½ Tbsp. ginger
¼ c. orange juice
1 Tbsp. mineral water

Peel and seed mango. Rough chop mango and combine with remaining ingredients in blender. Puree until smooth, about 30 seconds. Remove from blender. Chill and reserve for service.

POMEGRANATE MIGNONETTE

MAKES ABOUT ½ CUP;
SERVING SIZE: 1 TEASPOON

¼ c. red wine vinegar
¼ c. pomegranate juice
1 Tbsp. chopped shallots
1½ tsp. cracked black pepper
1 tsp. extra-virgin olive oil
1 tsp. granulated cane sugar

Whisk all ingredients together. Refrigerate until ready to serve.

CALORIES: 120; TOTAL FAT: 3.5 G; CARBOHYDRATES: 8 G;
DIETARY FIBER: 0 G; PROTEIN: 14 G

HERB-ROASTED RACK OF LAMB with WILD BLUEBERRY–SUN-DRIED TOMATO COMPOTE and CHIPOTLE POLENTA

MAKES 4 SERVINGS

4 six-ounce New Zealand lamb chops (4–5 bones per rack), trimmed and frenched

1 tsp. fresh basil, chopped

1 tsp. fresh oregano, chopped

1 tsp. fresh thyme leaves

¼ tsp. fresh rosemary, chopped

¼ tsp. fresh tarragon, chopped

¼ tsp. kosher salt

⅛ tsp. freshly ground black pepper

2 tsp. Miraval Oil Blend (3:1 blend canola oil and extra-virgin olive oil)

1 recipe Wild Blueberry–Sun-Dried Tomato Compote (*recipe follows*)

1 recipe Chipotle Polenta (*recipe follows*)

Preheat the oven to 375°F.

Lightly season the lamb on all sides with the fresh chopped herbs and the salt and pepper.

Heat a large skillet or sauté pan over high heat. Add the oil and when hot, add the lamb in batches and cook, turning until well browned, 3 to 4 minutes per side.

Transfer the meat to a heavy baking sheet or roasting pan, and roast to desired temperature, 12 to 15 minutes for medium-rare.

Place the racks on a large cutting board and let rest for 2 to 3 minutes. While lamb is resting, make the polenta.

Using a heavy sharp knife, cut the racks into two 2-bone chops each, and fan over the polenta. Spoon the compote over the meat, and serve immediately.

CALORIES: 476; TOTAL FAT 11 G; CARBOHYDRATE 60 G; DIETARY FIBER: 3 G; PROTEIN 30 G

WILD BLUEBERRY–SUN-DRIED TOMATO COMPOTE

MAKES ABOUT 1 CUP; SERVINGS: 8; SERVING SIZE: 2 TABLESPOONS

2 tsp. shallots, julienned

½ tsp. Miraval Oil Blend (3:1 mix of canola oil and extra-virgin olive oil)

1 tsp. packed sun-dried tomatoes, julienned

3 Tbsp. raspberry liqueur

3 Tbsp. cabernet sauvignon or zinfandel

1 c. frozen blueberries

½ c. plus 1½ Tbsp. veal or beef stock

1 tsp. Chinese five spice, ground

½ tsp. cornstarch mixed with ½ tsp. cold water

In small sauce pot, sauté shallots in oil to release aroma and flavor, about 30 seconds, then add sun-dried tomatoes and continue to sauté for 1 minute.

Pour raspberry liqueur and wine into the pot to deglaze; reduce until liquid is almost evaporated, about 1 minute 30 seconds.

Add in two-thirds of the blueberries, the stock, and the five-spice blend. Bring to a simmer, about 2 minutes.

Slowly mix in cornstarch and water. Simmer until mixture is thick enough to coat the back of a spoon, about 3½ minutes.

Remove from heat, and add in remaining blueberries. Keep warm until ready to serve.

CHIPOTLE POLENTA

MAKES ABOUT 1 CUP

1 c. skim milk

¼ c. quick-cooking polenta

1 tsp. canned chipotle chili, minced

1 tsp. fresh rosemary, chopped

Bring milk to a simmer in a small thick-bottomed saucepan over medium heat. Add polenta, reduce heat, and stir until thick, about 3 minutes. Fold in chipotle and rosemary, and season to taste. Serve immediately.

INDEX OF RECIPES

Baked Apple Tortelli   54

Buffalo Carpaccio with Arugula Salad   118

Butternut Squash Risotto   150

Chimichurri Wild Sockeye Salmon with Risotto and Smoky Romesco Sauce   37

Fruit Energizer Smoothie   71

Herb-Roasted Rack of Lamb with Wild Blueberry–Sun-Dried Tomato Compote and Chipotle Polenta   200

Oysters on the Half Shell with Mango-Ginger Cocktail Sauce and Pomegranate Mignonette   197

Pan-Seared Diver Scallop with Purple Potatoes, Chives, and White Truffle Oil   21

Pan-Seared Duck with Granny Smith Apple and Chipotle Chutney   182

Pistachio-Mushroom Duxelles Stuffed Roasted Poblano Chili with Red Pepper Coulis   101

Prickly Pear Barbecue-Glazed Pork Tenderloin with Grilled Watermelon   135

Quinoa Salad in Radicchio Cups   86

Vegetarian Black Bean Soup   167

Wild Salmon Crostini with Agave-Thyme Vinaigrette   198

ACKNOWLEDGMENTS

As a result of our guest response and the creative process for the previously released *Mindful Eating* cookbook, our talented Miraval Wellness and Spa professionals began to formulate *Mindful Living* as a way to provide educational information, healthy recipes, spa services, and practical tools to help our guests and readers make choices to live better lives. With mindfulness as our core philosophy and with our loyal guests and fans in mind, we hope to inspire others to live in the moment.

Miraval wishes to expressly thank the many professional and support staff at Miraval Resort & Spa in Tucson for making this book come to life, especially Brent Baum, Lauren Bloch, Tim Frank, Ahmad Ghemrawi, Brenda Helps, Larry Lamy, Pam Lancaster, Chad Luethje, Junelle Lupiani, Kim Macy, Justin Macy, Simon Marxer, Neil McLeod, Mary Monaghan, Jim Nicolai, MaryGrace Naughton, Anne Parker, Nicole Roseland, Carol Stratford, Tejpal, Michael Tompkins, Pam Trudeau, Wyatt Webb, Leigh Weinraub, Andrew Wolf, and Kris Wright.

Additionally, Miraval is grateful for our partnership contributions and would like to thank Clarins Skincare; Andrew Weil, M.D.; and Richard Baxter.

With each new book, Miraval has had the support of our owners, Steve and Jean Case; our Chairman of the Board, Philippe Bourguignon; the Miraval Board; and our publisher, Hay House. We are grateful for their unwavering commitment to further the mission of Miraval, which is to simply teach our guests to live in the present moment.

Miraval also wishes to thank Kim Wright Wiley for her writing abilities, interviewing skills, and patience through this process. Without Kim's fortitude in seeking us out to share her idea, this compilation would not have come to life.

Finally, from our entire Miraval family, we hope the lessons found in *Mindful Living* encourage you, the reader, to take life's journey one glorious step at a time!

We hope you enjoyed this Hay House book. If you'd like to receive our online catalog featuring additional information on Hay House books and products, or if you'd like to find out more about the Hay Foundation, please contact:

Hay House, Inc., P.O. Box 5100, Carlsbad, CA 92018-5100
(760) 431-7695 or (800) 654-5126
(760) 431-6948 (fax) or (800) 650-5115 (fax)
www.hayhouse.com® • www.hayfoundation.org

Published and distributed in Australia by: Hay House Australia Pty. Ltd., 18/36 Ralph St., Alexandria NSW 2015 • *Phone:* 612-9669-4299 • *Fax:* 612-9669-4144 • www.hayhouse.com.au

Published and distributed in the United Kingdom by: Hay House UK, Ltd., 292B Kensal Rd., London W10 5BE • *Phone:* 44-20-8962-1230 • *Fax:* 44-20-8962-1239 • www.hayhouse.co.uk

Published and distributed in the Republic of South Africa by: Hay House SA (Pty), Ltd., P.O. Box 990, Witkoppen 2068 • *Phone/Fax:* 27-11-467-8904 • www.hayhouse.co.za

Published in India by: Hay House Publishers India, Muskaan Complex, Plot No. 3, B-2, Vasant Kunj, New Delhi 110 070 • *Phone:* 91-11-4176-1620 • *Fax:* 91-11-4176-1630 • www.hayhouse.co.in

Distributed in Canada by: Raincoast, 9050 Shaughnessy St., Vancouver, B.C. V6P 6E5 • *Phone:* (604) 323-7100 • *Fax:* (604) 323-2600 • www.raincoast.com

Take Your Soul on a Vacation

Visit **www.HealYourLife.com**® to regroup, recharge,
and reconnect with your own magnificence.
Featuring blogs, mind-body-spirit news, and life-changing
wisdom from Louise Hay and friends.

VISIT WWW.HEALYOURLIFE.COM TODAY!

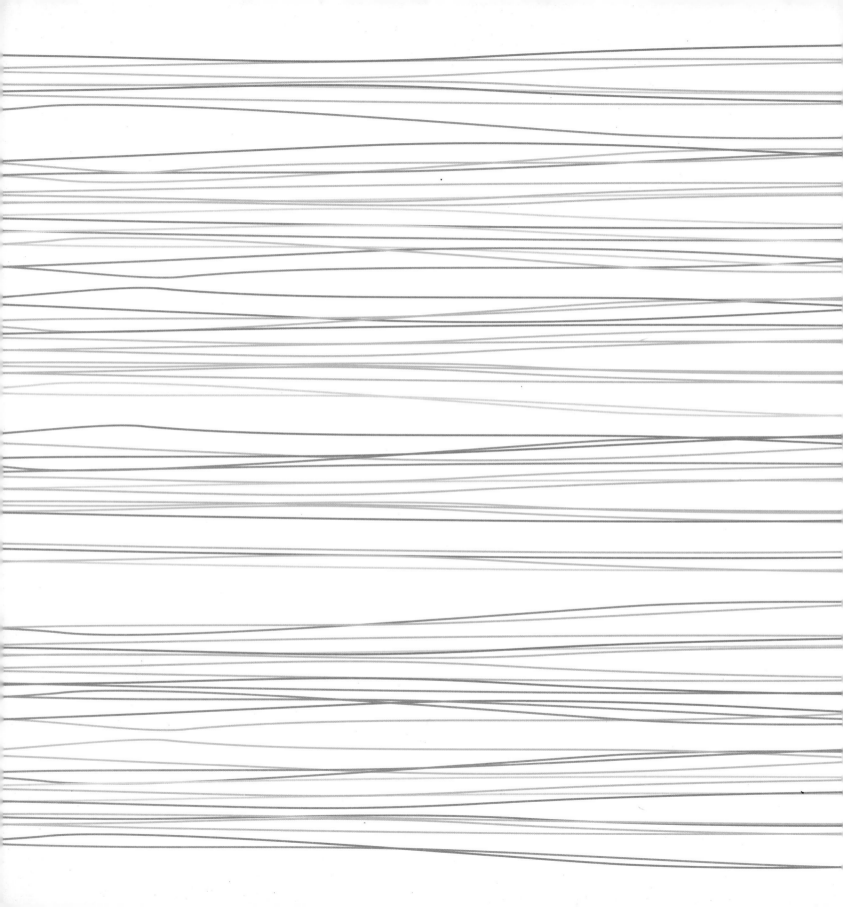